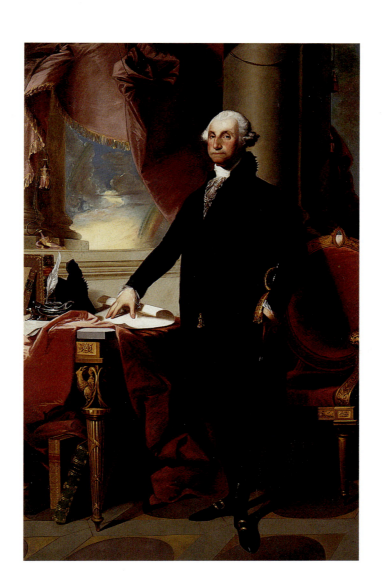

From Strength to Strength

A PICTORIAL HISTORY OF
THE GEORGE WASHINGTON UNIVERSITY
1821-1996

Published by
The George Washington University

Acknowledgements

The George Washington University
175th Anniversary
HONORARY CHAIRS

John D. Zeglis
Chairman, Board of Trustees

Oliver T. Carr, Jr.
Chairman Emeritus, Board of Trustees

Stephen Joel Trachtenberg
President

175TH ANNIVERSARY HISTORY BOOK
ADVISORY COMMITTEE

Roderick S. French
*Chair and Former Vice President
for Academic Affairs*

Jerome Barron
Professor of Law

Walter M. Bortz III
*Vice President for Administrative and
Information Services*

Sandy Holland
Executive Director of University Relations

Allan B. Weingold
*Vice President for Medical Affairs,
Executive Dean and Chairman of
the Governing Board of the Medical
Faculty Associates*

Michael J. Worth
*Vice President for Development and
Alumni Affairs*

Produced by the Office of
the 175th Anniversary

Director
Christopher Speron

Project Manager
Chris M. Kormis

Executive Editor
Sandy Holland

Researchers
Werner Steger, *Principal Researcher*
William McClenahan, Jr.

University Archives
G. David Anderson, Dagne Yemam,
Karen Greisman, Beth Palubinskas and staff

Editorial Assistant
Sam Silverstein

Design
Frank Glickman, Inc.
Frank Glickman and Matthew Monk

Production Coordinator
Susan McNally

Printing
Strine Printing Company, Inc.

We offer special thanks to the 175th Publications
Committee, whose stellar work provided invaluable
guidance and direction.

Finally, we wish to thank the GW Department
of History for its help in writing the text of this
book—help which provided both substance and
vitality to the words you are about to read.

From Strength to Strength
A Pictorial History of The George Washington University
1821-1996

For information:
The George Washington University
Office of University Relations
2121 Eye Street, NW
Suite 512
Washington, DC 20052

Printed in The United States of America

LIBRARY OF CONGRESS CATALOGING-IN-PUBLICATION DATA
George Washington University.
From strength to strength: a pictorial history of
the George Washington University, 1821-1996 /
George Washington University.
p.   cm.
Includes bibliographical references and index.
ISBN 0-9648258-0-5 (hardcover).
1. George Washington University–History–Pictorial works.
I. Title.
LD1933.G46   1995
378.753—dc20   95-35850
                                                      CIP

Contents

Prologue: The Work at Hand

This university has weathered a great deal in the course of 175 years in Washington: there is thunder—and brilliant sunshine, too—in the pages of this book you hold in your hands now. It is not my intention to steal either from this narrative of GW's history or to diminish your joy of discovery as you read it, but some truths go to the heart of the matter and are sturdy enough to bear repetition.

In the first few pages, you will read this plain statement about the early days of Columbian College: "The College would ultimately find its 'endowment' in its location." What was ultimately true for Columbian, the penniless foster child passed back and forth between its Baptist parents and the United States Congress, has also proven true for The George Washington University, now somewhat prosperous and self governing in its maturity.

Whether we have lived from hand to mouth or relatively well, there has been one constant in our history: we have always been here in Washington, in the Capital City. We have moved from College Hill, just north of old Boundary Street, now Florida Avenue, to Foggy Bottom with several stops along the way. We have occupied the buildings of others, been evicted from a few, built our own, and, to close the circle, built some for others to occupy.

From the infancy of Washington, when it was a mud puddle and a backwater entitling diplomats to hardship pay, to the emergence of Washington as the capital of the greatest power in the world, it has been our good fortune—our endowment or our patrimony, if you will—to ripen and grow up hand in hand with the city of our birth.

Good fortune, indeed. But we have always capitalized on what was near to hand. Perhaps this is the greatest lesson of this present history of GW.

Propinquity alone must never be taken for granted as the one sure characteristic of success. Otherwise, no institution, educational or commercial, would ever have failed in Washington, though many have foundered in the last 175 years. Location, our endowment, has always been a resource to be exploited and refined, like gold, and just as precious.

Our historical and capital strength has been to reach out our hand to the men and women who came to Washington for the excitement of its politics, law, and diplomacy. More than the institutions they served, the bureaucrats, lawyers, engineers, and military officers were the government's resources, but also the city's capital. By enabling them to add value to their lives and careers through further education—often at night or part time and on the fly—both Columbian College and The George

Washington University enriched themselves. But no less did they enrich the nation and this cosmopolitan mass of public servants—judges, legislators, members of the Joint Chiefs, and diplomats—many of whom later returned the favor when they came back to Columbian or GW to teach.

Nor were they the only ones. The excitement of the city, especially since the end of the Civil War when we ceased to be a characteristically "southern" institution, has attracted the young from all over America and, more recently, from all around the world. We have profited from the good fortune of our geography in the coin of diversity and an ever-increasing excellence in both faculty and students—profited even when we may have thought otherwise.

During the student unrest of the late 1960s and 1970s, GW was not itself a hotbed of student radicalism, but was—at a seven-minute walk from The White House—a good place to bunk for the night and a handy staging area for the protest or (lamentably) the riot the next day. Yet, I hasten to add that misgivings about these events, or any events in our history, must yield to an understanding that they were inevitable in Washington and, therefore, part of the continued parallel growth of GW with that of the city.

The transforming and the traditional—the radicals no less than the bureaucrats—have always been part of the mix and near at hand. We have reached out and grasped the opportunities that our

fortunate location has placed nearby—but gently, to hold them and make them grow.

Cloyd Heck Marvin, whose tenure from 1927 to 1959 was the longest of any GW president, made roses grow in the University Yard. He was a builder too—of faculty, enrollments, and the rather utilitarian structures of GW's campus. But he grew himself—we might say he grew into Washington—and over a period of years his conservative belief that the University should stay at arm's length from government and its money woke up to the new realities of living in the new Washington of World War II and the postwar era.

The nearness to government with its enormous research needs and, after the war, the great influx of students on the G.I. Bill convinced President Marvin to accept the fundamental truth of the University's history. Without a policy of cooperation with the government next door and without accepting government research projects, the University would be diminished, but with them his handiwork of bigger buildings and enrollments would remain robust.

To say that his successors, Thomas Henry Carroll, Lloyd Hartman Elliott, and I, profited at least as much from his willingness to capitalize on the changes in Washington as from his new buildings is to state only part of the truth. The University we know today would not be so well endowed in all senses had he not had the entrepreneurial spirit to make the most of our natural endowment, our location, two generations ago.

We are used to reading, carved into the stone of the National Archives, that "What is past is prologue." It is also, I believe, prediction. Marvin's successor, President Carroll, who died prematurely and served only four years, broadened the enterprising nature of GW as he turned to a long-neglected part of the city: its public schools, which he believed GW's education school could serve better, and its black population. As Marvin's turn toward formal relations with the federal government may be said to have predicted Carroll's enterprising initiatives, so Carroll's hand extended to African Americans through education may be accurately seen to have predicted Lloyd Elliott's Educational Opportunities Program for black students and, later in 1988, our educational and financial commitment to the 21st Century Scholars Program of scholarships for promising graduates of Washington's predominantly black high schools.

Making good on predictions implies continuity. The changing life and events in Washington have always been anticipatory of the University's response and truly predictive of its immediate future. In the case of Lloyd Elliott, I should amend this modest truism and declare that his acting in harmony with the rhythm of the Capital City has helped to ensure the long-term future health of GW.

President Elliott was a builder like President Marvin, but truly an entrepreneur. The campus grew under his presidency and so did its endowment—

from $9 million in 1965 to $250 million when he retired in 1988. Yet in keeping with our history, Lloyd Elliott built the financial endowment by investing, quite literally, in our endowment of location, in booming downtown Washington's real estate. The buildings he built housed our classrooms and offices, but also commercial enterprises and offices, the rents from which have funded additional campus projects and will continue to strengthen the University and keep it agile and responsive in the face of change.

This is some of what has been handed down to us—there is so much more to read in the text and to see in images on the following pages. But there is no question that the series of predictions, only a few of which I have touched on, is not about to be broken. How could it be? The growth of the University and the particular accomplishments of past presidents, professors, and students all return us to the same lesson. Our location is our patrimony and our capital, and we will continue to prosper only if we keep them in hand and never let them fall through our fingers, never lose touch with this city and our place in it.

Some years ago, in a fit of obscure thought, someone proposed to President Elliott that GW should aim to become Harvard on the Potomac. To his eternal credit and as testimony to his understanding of this university, Elliott dismissed the notion. It is as preposterous as aiming to transform Harvard into

George Washington on the Charles— and no less preposterous, or indigestible, as a failure of imagination, given our past and our present.

With the State Department on our doorstep, we have no need to look north or to any other point of the compass to stake our claim in international relations. With a large and permanent contingent provided by Washington's diplomatic community, we need no special license to profit from the globalism we preach and admire today. And with Washington's multicultural population, diversity and local talent come naturally and easily to us.

All this is at hand, and so are 3,500 associations, businesses of every size and description, men and women of ambition and talent. We need to be enterprising in extending our reach and to profit from our neighbors as they continue to profit from us. And we need one more thing: we need, as I believe I am reported in this history to have said, to love ourselves more. GW must proceed with every confidence that it can be—because it is already in many cases—the best university for certain things and first rate for everything else.

After 175 years, we have become more than the faithful handmaiden of the Capital City: as we have grown larger and more comprehensive, we have also grown to be inseparably part of it. We are here to stay. We are a landmark in Washington, attractive, even magnetic. When Hillary Rodham Clinton wanted to make the case for health-care reform, she came to us. When Václav Havel, the

Czech hero, made his one public address in the United States in April of 1993, he came to us. When Abba Eban wanted to turn his hand to teaching in Washington, he came to us.

They came to us and honored us in coming no less than the old generations of students and professors honored us with their presence and faith, and no less than the new generations honor us now as they arrive year after year. The honors, I expect, will continue to flow to us in Washington and so will inevitable challenges. Both are in our past and so, we may predict, will be in our future—yet this is cause for optimism. The thunderstorms that have hardened the Capital City and the sunshine that has made it grow have also made GW hardy and flourishing since 1821.

Nothing in our history of learning and service contradicts this proposition, and in truth the written and pictorial history of GW you have in hand validates it and predicts a brilliant future across the next 175 years.

Stephen Joel Trachtenberg

Stephen Joel Trachtenberg
President and Professor of
Public Administration

Buildings on College Hill,
adjoining the City of Washington, in
the District of Columbia.—

A Building sufficiently spacious for
the accommodation of a hundred Students,
and two others for the accommodation of
Professors, are erecting, and funds, needed
for their completion, are respectfully solicited
Subscriptions will be thankfully received
and faithfully applied: and it is believed
they will contribute to the national welfare.

Luther Rice. Ag.t

The above is recommended by.

Wm H Crawford

J. C. Calhoun

Sam.l H Smallwood

Josiah Meigs

Jn.o Peter

R. Meigs &
Students

Hopes and Aspirations in the Nation's Capital

BEGINNINGS

The University as we have come to know it began in 1821 as Columbian College, a small, underfunded, and neglected stepchild of its Baptist founders, a group of clergymen who from the outset produced more enthusiasm than endowment. The College also did not receive much financial encouragement from the fledgling federal government, its neighbor and most obvious beneficiary. To make matters worse, when Congress insisted on giving the College a non-sectarian charter, it diminished whatever incentive the Baptists might have had to develop a strong proprietary interest. By 1904, the Baptist affiliation, always tenuous, had disappeared. And later Congresses never quite embraced the Washington-Adams vision of funding as well as chartering "a great national university."

Left without external resources, the College would ultimately find its endowment in its location. Its capital would accumulate as the capital city came more fully to appreciate having a nearby educational institution unswervingly responsive to its needs. Beginning in 1821, however, this someday University would struggle for more

than a century to find enough straw to reinforce its bricks. Hence the title, *Bricks Without Straw*, used by University Historian Elmer Kayser in 1971 to describe the University's prolonged financial ordeal.

James Monroe had scarcely begun his second term when Congress on February 9, 1821, chartered Columbian College. Classes began promptly the first week in September when 11 freshmen met with Irah Chase, a professor of theology. Such beginnings were the norm, for even without Baptist sponsorship, theological training typified the core curriculum of small colleges like Columbian in an era when an educated clergy was seen as indispensable to maintaining civilized society. Would-be lawyers might still prepare for the bar by "reading law," but carrying God and the Gospel to the frontier was a mission too sacred to be left to the untutored.

A semester later, classics joined theology when on January 9, 1822, Columbian fielded a classical department, thereby rounding out what passed for a liberal arts curriculum in the young republic. Columbian students, we might note, like the men who had recently

(Left) President James Monroe signed the charter and attended the first commencement. Relations with the federal government remained an important part of GW's history.

(Below) Receipt to the Rev. Obadiah Bruen Brown, the first president of the Board of Trustees of the College, from Luther Rice, founder of Columbian College.

drafted a Constitution, saw nothing anomalous in preparing themselves for public or private careers by studying such "irrelevant"
subjects as moral philosophy, theology, Greek, and Latin. Indeed,
Latin was to remain required of all bachelor of arts candidates
until 1908. Its passing is still lamented in some quarters.

Columbian's matriculants had grown from 11 to 30 by the time
the winter term began in January 1822. They were not a passive
lot. In March, they organized GW's oldest student activity—the
Enosinian debating society—defunct today, but so effusive in its
prime that when (16 years later) it began to publish its proceedings,
its collected works ultimately totaled 1,800 volumes.

Columbian College held its first graduation on December 15, 1824,
a ceremony that took place in a Presbyterian church where the
Willard Hotel now stands. Here fittingly the man whom George
Washington looked upon as the son he never had—the aging
Marquis de Lafayette—on his last visit to his adopted country,
shared the stage with President John Quincy Adams and members
of Adams' cabinet. Ever since 1824, the tradition has lived on.
Whether an Adams, a McKinley, a Kennedy, or a Hillary Rodham
Clinton, national dignitaries have been on stage at key moments of
GW's history.

*A student's account covering all
expenses for a term, 1825.*

*The original College building
on College Hill, constructed
1820-1822.*

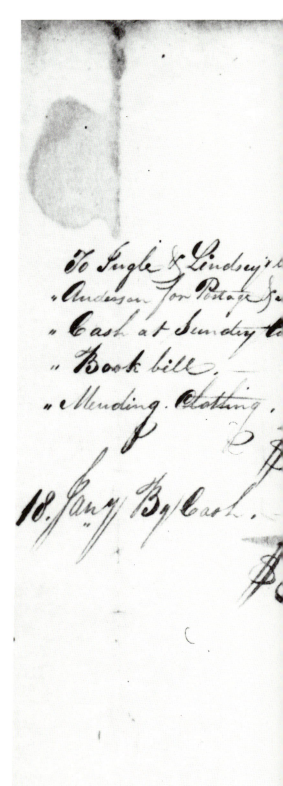

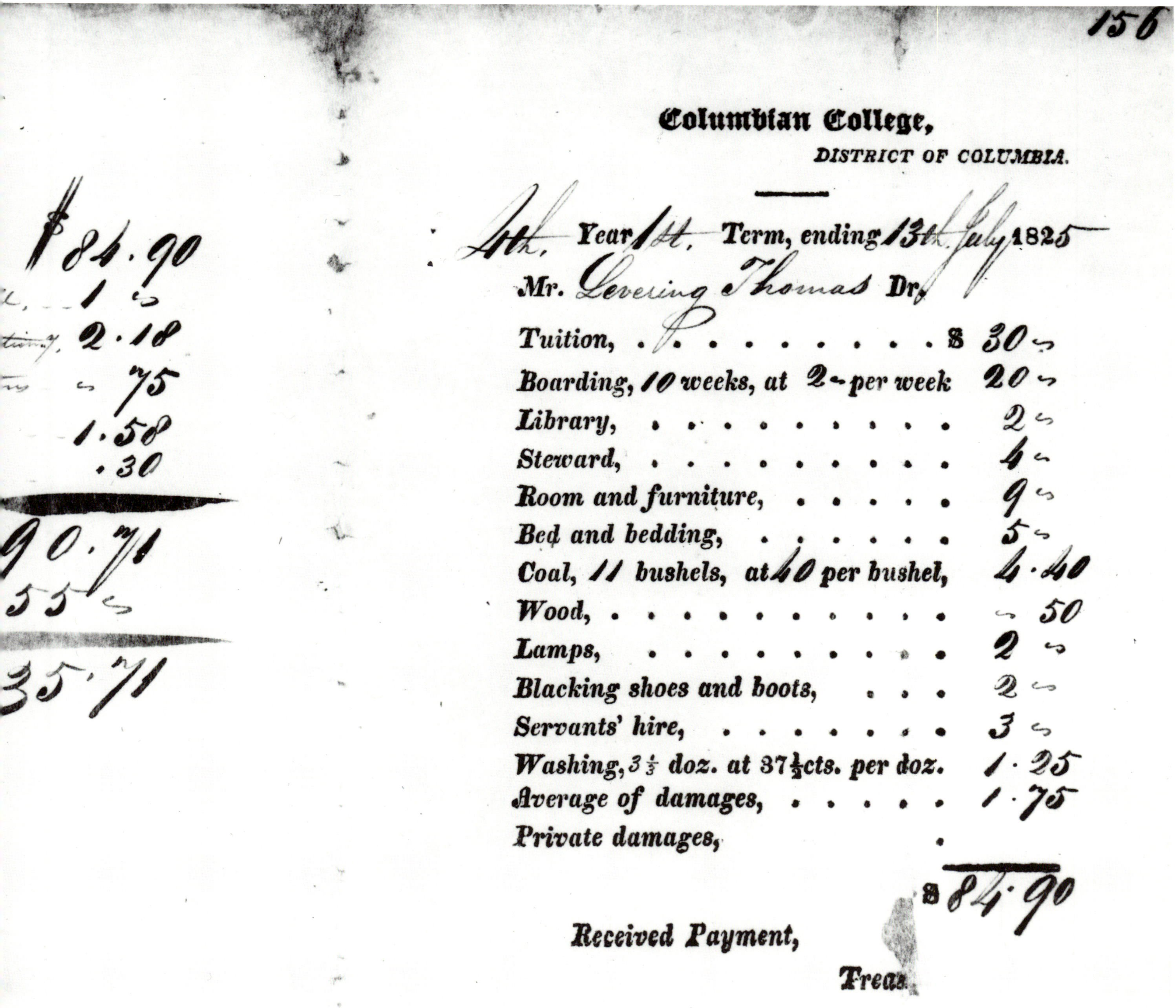

156

$ 84.90

1

2·18

75

1·58

·30

90·71

55

35·71

Columbian College,

DISTRICT OF COLUMBIA.

———

4th. Year *1st.* Term, ending *13th July* 1825

Mr. *Levering Thomas* Dr.

Tuition, ...	$ 30
Boarding, *10* weeks, at *2* per week	20
Library, ...	2
Steward, ...	4
Room and furniture, ...	9
Bed and bedding, ...	5
Coal, *11* bushels, at *40* per bushel,	4·40
Wood, ...	50
Lamps, ...	2
Blacking shoes and boots, . .	2
Servants' hire, ...	3
Washing, 3⅓ doz. at 37½cts. per doz.	1·25
Average of damages, ...	1·75
Private damages, .	
	$ 84·90

Received Payment,

Treas.

*William Staughton, first president,
1821-1827.*

THE MEDICAL SCHOOL BEGINS

Cadavers were hard to come by when Columbian's new medical department opened in March 1825. This may explain why no particular disrepute attached to the department head whose recent brush with Massachusetts authorities over a charge of body-snatching ended quietly when a rising lawyer named Daniel Webster got him off. Medical students, meanwhile, met classes in what was described as a commodious building at 10th and E Streets, NW. This downtown location, far from Columbian's main building on College Hill, also signaled the medical department's separateness in other ways. Not unlike its modern counterpart, GW's first "med school" had its own budget and was expected to be financially self-supporting. Highlighting its early history, Columbian had to fight off the efforts of Georgetown College to set up a competing medical school nearby. Ultimately, the case went from the courts to Congress which, in its wisdom, agreed that one medical school on this side of Rock Creek would suffice.

STRUGGLING TO SURVIVE

For the College as a whole, ups and downs tended to come in swift succession. Good news broke in the spring of 1826 when a group of influential Baptists meeting in New York City announced their intention to subscribe $50,000 to help pay off part of the College debt. And, on the academic front that spring, William Cranch, distinguished jurist and reporter of Supreme Court decisions, held classes in what proved to be our first, but short-lived, law school.

The bad news arrived a year later. Due perhaps to overexpansion, financial shortages forced the College to suspend classes from May 1827 to May 1828. Only a handful of students remaining loyally in residence was on hand when classes resumed for a three-month session in the summer of 1828. What role Congress may have played in rescuing the College at this time can only be surmised, but its willingness to cancel $30,000 of College debt in exchange for deeds to College property on Greenleaf's Point doubtless helped revive Columbian's flagging finances. By September, classes had returned to the normal cycle of fall and spring semesters. The nascent law department appears to have been the major casualty. Although the College offered occasional law classes thereafter, the degree has been conferred continuously only since 1865.

The federal government did not entirely ignore its neighbor's financial distress. In July 1832, as it prepared to wrestle with a nullification crisis in South Carolina, Congress conveyed 180 saleable house lots to the College, stipulating only that the proceeds be used for endowment and debt reduction. Originally assessed at a value of $25,000, these lots (all but 10 of them) had been sold off by 1910 for approximately $71,000. Like inviting dignitaries to commencements, securing endowment by real estate transaction would become another tradition in the life of the University.

Continued on p. 20

The Medical School

REMOTE ORIGINS

In 1825, four years after its founding, Columbian College added a medical department. At the time, there was only a distant connection between medical education and the clinical practice of medicine. The modern hospital had not yet been invented. Populated by the poor, not the rich, hospitals in the early 19th century bore a closer resemblance to poorhouses than they did to centers for the practice of surgery. As historian Charles Rosenberg has written, "the hospital was something Americans of the better sort did for their less fortunate countrymen; it was hardly a refuge they contemplated entering themselves."

The medical department opened with what University Archivist David Anderson describes as a first-rate faculty, which included Thomas Sewall, a professor of anatomy and a Harvard graduate, and James Staughton. It offered what at the time constituted a full curriculum—anatomy, physiology, surgery, "theory and practice of physic," materia medica, chemistry, and obstetrics.

In 1844, the medical department moved to what was supposed to have been an insane asylum. In fact, the Washington Infirmary on Judiciary Square had a pedigree not unlike that of other 19th-century hospitals. Congress had purchased the building in 1806 and

promptly turned it into a poorhouse. Later it served as a jail, and still later Congress decided to make it over into yet another kind of asylum. After the building was renovated to become an insane asylum, a great public outcry among local residents caused Congress to abandon the project.

Instead of an insane asylum, the building became an infirmary, something regarded as more benign. Hence, in 1844, the GW Infirmary began operation as the first general hospital in the nation's capital. The medical department thereby gained a teaching hospital, long before most medical schools could claim such an amenity.

In 1847, the school changed its name to the National Medical College and continued to serve non-paying patients who

(From the top) The first building of the medical department (1826-1834 and 1839-1844), stood on the northeast corner of 10th and E Streets. After GW sold the building, it was used for commercial purposes, as shown. These surroundings gave little hint of what the medical school was to become.

10th Street, about the turn of the century, showing Ford's Theatre and, at the corner of 10th and E Streets, the medical school.

NATIONAL MEDICAL COLLEGE.

(Above) The medical school, on the north side of H Street, midway between 13th and 14th Streets. In 1865, while being used as the U.S. Army Medical Museum, William Wilson Corcoran offered this building to the College. The building became the medical school for two years, 1866-1868.

(Right) Washington Infirmary in Judiciary Square. An early teaching hospital, it housed the medical school from 1844-1861.

(Far right) Destruction of the infirmary by fire, 1861.

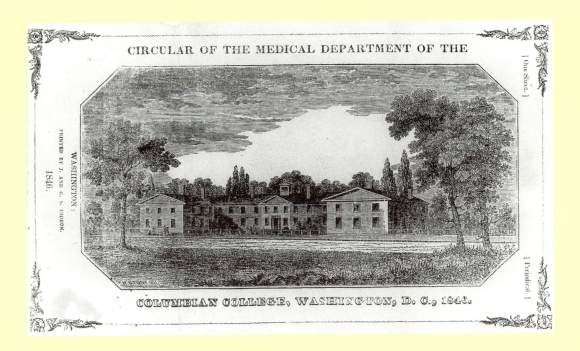

CIRCULAR OF THE MEDICAL DEPARTMENT OF THE

[One Sheet.]

WASHINGTON: PRINTED BY J. AND G. S. GIDEON. 1846.

[Periodical.]

COLUMBIAN COLLEGE, WASHINGTON, D. C., 1845.

lacked a residence that would have allowed them to receive home care. Every year Congress appropriated up to $6,000 for the treatment of "transient sick paupers."

The GW Infirmary was enlarged in 1853, in response to growing need. The infirmary and the medical school prospered in the 1850s, but the College lost control of the infirmary during the Civil War when it was converted to a military hospital. The infirmary never reverted back to the College. Instead, it burned to the ground in November 1861.

Doctors affiliated with GW played a prominent role in the Civil War. Dr. Alexander Y.P. Garnett, who had served as a professor of anatomy since 1854, became Jefferson Davis's personal physician in Richmond. Abraham Lincoln received medical attention from Dr. Robert King Stone, who also had taught at GW.

During the war and afterwards, the medical school moved from place to place within the city and operated on the barest of margins. In 1868, the medical school received a new building at 1335 H Street from W.W. Corcoran, philanthropist and president of GW's Board of Trustees from 1869 to 1888. Reporting in August 1868, the *Evening Express* described Corcoran's gift as a place for students to "practice application of bandages and surgical appliances, to use the microscope, and to practice on the manikin."

In the period between 1866 and 1903, medical education took place primarily in the late afternoon and evening. That permitted students to hold jobs elsewhere in the city and allowed GW to attract some first-rate talent from other institutions for medical instruction. Walter Reed, famous for his work on the pathology of yellow fever and for whom the nation's major military hospital would be named, lectured at GW. So did Dr. Frederick Russell, who introduced typhoid vaccine into the Army and Dr. A.F.A. King, whose *Manual of Obstetrics* was the standard at that time. In 1893, the University instituted a four-year course in medicine.

The first female student entered the school of medicine in 1884. When that student graduated in 1887, Professor Coues, speaking at the commencement ceremonies held at the Congregational Church, noted that, "This is the sixty-fifth annual commencement of the National Medical College. Which means, among other things, that it has taken the Medical Department of Columbian University more than three-score years to grow wise enough to secure what was needed—a woman graduate. Now it only takes a woman three years to secure what she may desire: a diploma."

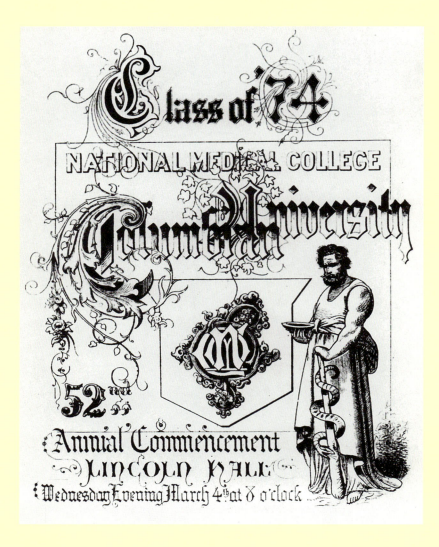

(Above) Walter Reed lectured at GW.

(Left) Memorabilia from the 1874 medical school commencement.

By 1990, the gender balance had shifted significantly. For the first time in the institution's history, the number of women enrolled in The George Washington University School of Medicine and Health Sciences outnumbered men. In 1995, women represented 52 percent of the entering class.

A MODERN MEDICAL SCHOOL

In 1882 the University built a preparatory school just west of the medical school. When the school closed in 1897, its building became the site of the new University Hospital. The first patients entered the hospital in 1898. Once again, the medical school was united with a teaching hospital. Meanwhile, the medical school building was renovated in 1887, and a new building constructed in 1902. In 1931, the medical school added a brick annex to the H Street building to house laboratory facilities.

Medicine at GW in the first half of this century featured some spectacular advances. In the 1930s, Dr. Claude Moore established one of the nation's leading radiology departments. In the school's laboratories, Dr. Vincent du Vigneaud did most of the biochemical research that would earn him a Nobel Prize in chemistry in 1955. In 1970, Julius Axelrod, Ph.D., received a Nobel Prize in medicine.

The medical school acquired an excellent reputation as a place to train practicing physicians. It became known as a clinically based institution, in which even the basic sciences that students took in their first two years contained clinical components. One long-time faculty member noted that, "from the 1920s on through to the present, the medical school, if it stood for anything, stood for outstanding clinical training." GW graduates received prestigious internships and residencies because people knew that GW students were well trained and able to stand on their own.

Dr. Frank Miller, who graduated from the school in 1948, remembers the building at 1335 H Street that housed the school as dominated by a five-story stairwell. The elevator serving the school was so old that when it broke down, it required special parts and the attention of an Otis Elevator vice president to fix it. Medical students were not allowed on the elevator. Instead, they walked up and down the five flights of steps past banisters embellished with the letters "CU," which few realized stood for Columbian University.

As the students toiled on H Street, the relationship between GW's medical school and the city of Washington remained close. To serve the city better, GW President Cloyd Heck Marvin secured President Franklin D. Roosevelt's approval in September 1944 for the construction of a new hospital, to be built near Washington Circle. The government, utilizing extraordinary wartime appropriations, provided more than $4 million for the hospital's construction. On March 23, 1948, the University held a special convocation to dedicate the new hospital. At the ceremony, Major General Phillip B. Fleming, administrator of the Federal Works

Agency, formally presented the University with the new hospital which instantly became the most modern in Washington.

The new hospital continued to be a center for medical innovation. In 1956, GW purchased its first artificial kidney—a "Kolff Kidney" with the serial number "4"—to be used in acute treatments. In 1964, Professor Alvin Parrish (M.D.'45) opened Washington's first non-military dialysis unit—establishing a tradition of progressive renal medicine that continues at GW today.

In 1966, the University dedicated the Eugene Meyer Pavilion, offering greatly increased laboratory, x-ray, research, and clinical treatment facilities. An entire floor of the Meyer Pavilion, devoted to research, housed the six-million-volt linear accelerator, the radioisotope laboratory, operating theaters with overhead observation galleries, and surgical suites for minor and oral surgery.

Even as the hospital evolved into a high-tech center for the practice of medicine, the medical school remained behind at 13th and H Streets, increasingly isolated from the rest of the campus. Students with clinical responsibilities trudged back and forth from their lectures to the hospital.

This isolation aside, GW students received a first-rate medical education. In the third year, the students left the laboratories and classrooms on H Street and spent most of their time in hospital clerkships. Rotating through the internal medicine, pediatrics, obstetrics and gynecology, and psychiatry departments, students learned the essentials of clinical medicine. They took medical histories of the astonishingly diverse array of patients and performed medical examinations.

GW medical students worked long and demanding hours, as did the interns and residents who assisted in the clinical teaching.

(Above) The University Hospital, 1898-1948.

(Right) On March 23, 1948, the University dedicated the current hospital, which became the most modern facility in Washington.

*Medical students prepare for class
in Hall A on H Street.*

In the new facilities, old problems related to the financing of medicine remained to be resolved. The medical school was as complex an entity as any within the University, since it involved both professional training and the actual provision of care. Within the school, considerable debates occurred over how the faculty's time should be divided between clinical and research duties and over how much the hospital and medical school should rely on permanent staff, rather than on practicing physicians who taught on a part-time basis.

By 1970, new concepts, such as managed care, and new institutions, such as the health maintenance organization, had entered the medical scene. The medical school community found itself on the cusp of change. One doctor, who came to GW in 1970 from the National Institutes of Health, described the institution as one "starved of new, young faculty for a long time." But, that changed in the 1970s, in part because of the "new people who were coming in and...the enthusiasm that new programs, new people, new ideas kept generating."

REAGAN

The newly energized institution received national attention on March 30, 1981. On the 70th day of his presidency, Ronald Reagan underwent three hours of emergency surgery at the University Hospital to remove the bullet that had

REJOINING THE CAMPUS

In May 1973, the medical school rejoined the rest of the campus with the gala dedication of the Walter G. Ross Hall and the Paul Himmelfarb Health Sciences Library. C.A. Beeck, who worked as a security guard at the medical school, expressed the feelings of many when he noted that the new location made the old one "look like a barn." No longer would GW medical students study in a place that contained only one elevator and be forced to run "up and down the steps like ants on an anthill."

The new library constituted a major improvement, with audiovisual equipment and related learning facilities that were "as modern as any medical library in the country," according to Daniel Yett of the library staff. In the old space, he said, "every inch of space was used. Books were actually stacked on the floor."

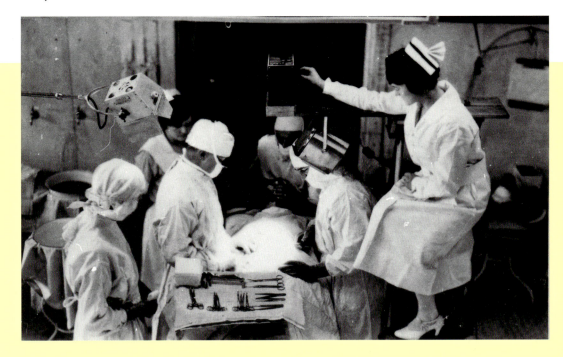

Those were the days:
(Above) An operating room in the old University hospital.

(Center) An x-ray facility at the University hospital. Virginia Stillman (left) and Eva Martins adjust 500-milliampere x-ray equipment, 1948.

(Below) Anatomy lab at the medical school on H Street.

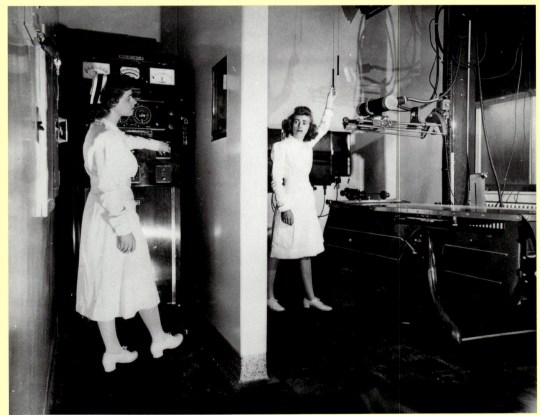

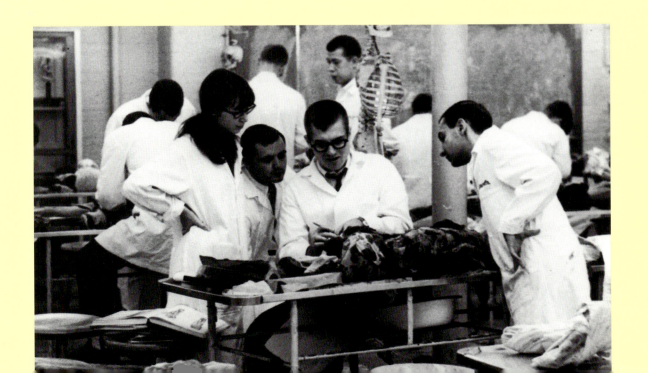

entered under his left armpit, struck his seventh rib, and burrowed three inches into his left lung. Drs. Benjamin Aaron and Joseph Giordano completed the surgery, and, by 7:25 p.m., Dr. Dennis O'Leary, the dean of clinical affairs, informed the press and the nation that Reagan's prognosis was excellent.

The reporters in Ross Hall had been waiting for hours to receive some news. "I've lectured in that room many times," O'Leary said, "but when I walked there [that] night, it was the most unreal sight, all those lights and instruments and cameras…a lot different from a lecture." As *The Washington Post* noted, O'Leary, like Reagan, came through the crisis admirably, facing down and taming a "near-ugly" press corps. And when he raised his arm to demonstrate how the bullet had entered the president's body, O'Leary became a star. He

emerged, according to the *Post*, as "a symbol of calm and reassurance to a nationwide audience."

Dean Robert I. Keimowitz later called Reagan's surgery and hospital stay a "defining moment" for the institution. He emphasized, however, that, "the hospital did for the president what it would do for anyone with major trauma who showed up in GW's emergency room."

The hospital excelled in far more than the treatment of trauma. Under the leadership of Drs. Hugo Rizzoli, Edward Laws, and Laligam Sekhar, the Department of Neurosurgery has become what one veteran observer calls the "flagship" of the clinical services at the Medical Center. Its program of "skull-based surgery" draws patients from all over the world. Endoscopic surgery is another area in which GW has gained a national reputation, in part

because it maintains one of the country's most modern teaching laboratories in this field.

HEALTH POLICY, HEALTH PROBLEMS

The medical school has the advantage of working with other parts of the University on questions related to medical ethics and health care finance. Each of these areas has figured prominently in the work of the medical school during the 1990s.

In this decade, the nation has endured what many would consider a health care crisis. The rising cost of insurance premiums and the changing nature of the labor force have combined to leave many working Americans with no form of health insurance. At the same time, GW, like many urban hospitals, has neither the desire nor the right to turn away needy patients. The result has been an epidemic of uncompensated care. In fiscal 1989, for example, the GW hospital provided some $30 million worth of uncompensated care. "The hospital is bleeding too much," Vice President for Medical Affairs L. Thompson Bowles said. He sought financial assistance from the government of the District of Columbia, which faced its own financial and political crises.

In response to the problems of health care finance, First Lady Hillary Rodham Clinton launched a task force in 1993 to produce what ultimately became the president's health care reform bill. GW's Center for Health Policy played a leading role in the effort. In further support

President and Mrs. Ronald Reagan meet with the press after President Reagan received life-saving treatment at the GW Hospital following an assassination attempt in 1981.

of the project, the Robert Wood Johnson Foundation, the nation's leading medical philanthropy, gave GW a grant to coordinate a series of seminars. With GW's help, Mrs. Clinton and the members of her task force met with groups around the country and solicited their views on health care reform.

THE MEDICAL SCHOOL AT 170

Those who studied at GW in the 1990s entered a medical profession that bore no resemblance to that encountered by GW's medical students in the 19th century. The setting has changed, and the change continues. In 1988, for example, GW dedicated its new Ambulatory Care Center, whose modern clinical offices, surgical suites, oncology center, radiology labs, and pharmacy adjoin the renovated doctors' offices in the Burns Building.

The mission remains the same, and the results have been impressive. In 1995, the University looked back with pride on several years of high rankings among medical schools that train primary care physicians.

Whatever ethical and economic dilemmas exist in relation to health care, GW recognizes that these problems stem as much from medicine's successes as from its failures. Those who run GW's medical school believe that a need remains for doctors and allied health professionals with strong clinical backgrounds, and GW's School of Medicine and Health Sciences continues to maintain a strong commitment to meeting that need.

(Top) First Lady Hillary Rodham Clinton selected the GW campus as a forum to discuss health care reform in 1993.

GW's Ambulatory Care Center, which opened in 1988, contains clinical offices, surgical suites, an oncology center, radiology labs, and a pharmacy.

Continued from p. 10

EXTRACURRICULAR AFFAIRS

On College Hill, meanwhile, Columbian students did what students usually do when not in class. They partied, they roughhoused (no weapons allowed), and they organized sporting events. In 1860, seemingly oblivious to the slavery crisis, they pitched in and built a gymnasium. But like GW students in every age, enlivened by public issues so close to the center of national life, they embraced popular and sometimes unpopular causes. In 1847, for example, the College expelled one Henry J. Arnold for conspiring to free a slave owned by the College Steward. In light of the student body's largely southern makeup, Arnold's expulsion may have spared him a worse fate.

That same year, the medical department became the National Medical College and, for the first time, the alumni made their presence felt. On July 14, 1847, some 27 alumni founded the Alumni Association of the Columbian College and announced the endowment of a professorship as their first worthy project.

Faculty, too, began to claim a more active role, calling for curriculum changes to meet the needs of an increasingly industrial economy. It made no sense, they argued, to house math, science, and engineering in the classical department. In 1852, they urged the creation of a new department, one that would separate the sciences from the teaching of Greek and Latin. A school of engineering was not far in the future.

THE CIVIL WAR

The Civil War nearly wiped out Columbian College and at the same time underscored the symbiosis between the federal city and its private institutions. Within a year of the firing on Fort Sumter, the Union government had commandeered both the medical infirmary (where Judiciary Square is today) and the College Hill property. When fire leveled the infirmary in late 1861, the College Hill building itself became a hospital and, with 884 beds, served as one of the city's four major military hospitals throughout the war.

Despite sagging enrollments, Columbian professors continued to teach, often holding wartime classes in their homes. Columbian's medical students, meanwhile, took their training into combat. Forty-six of the school's medical graduates served in the Union army, 24 in the Confederate forces.

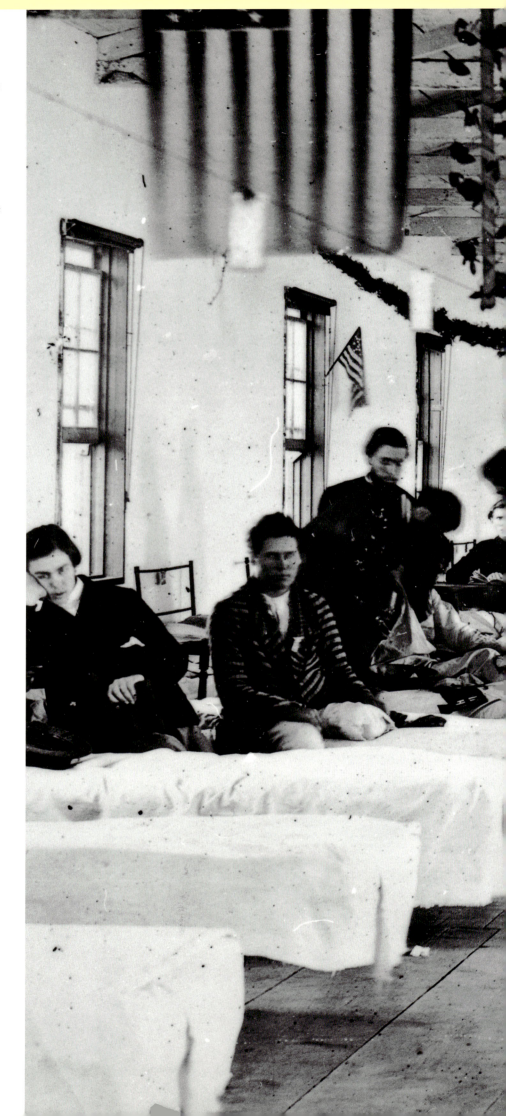

A Civil-War era convalescent ward in Columbian College General Hospital.

B-358

Lith. & Print by Chas. Magnus 12. Frankfort St. N.Y.

Entered according to act of Congress A.D. 1864 by Chas. Magnus in the Clerks Office of the S. District of New York.

CARVER BARRACKS, WASHING

TON, D.C.

(Left) Carver Barracks, on the site of the first campus of GW, housed Union soldiers during the Civil War. The original College building is the tall red brick building located left of the center.

(Above) During the Civil War, Matthew Brady photographed surgeons and hospital stewards stationed at the Washington Army hospitals.

Whether at home or in the field, the College community invariably found itself tied to the central events of its era. Not surprisingly, on April 12, 1865, Columbian College Professor of Surgery John F. May attended the death-bed of a president who had the ill-fortune not to have had access to the resources GW hospital was able to provide to Ronald Reagan 120 years later. In this instance, Professor May could do little but probe the wound and pronounce President Abraham Lincoln beyond medical help.

Curiously, Professor May was present at both ends of the assassination scenario. A few days after the tragedy at Ford's Theater, he was called to the Navy Yard to help identify the corpse of John Wilkes Booth. Because he had earlier removed a small tumor from the back of the actor's neck, May was satisfied that the scar he saw constituted a positive identification. Others, to this day, continue to harbor doubts.

RECONSTRUCTION

Bureaucracies swollen by war tend to resist shrinkage when peace returns. Post-Civil War Washington was no exception. Responding to the presence of a now-larger student pool, Columbian College began in the late 1860s to meet the needs of what might be called the "yumbies" of their day—those young, upwardly mobile bureaucrats who, striving for advancement, sought out Columbian's fast multiplying evening classes. With them came the part-time professors, many of them recruited from the higher ranks of the same civil service pool. Known today as academic "practitioners," these adjunct professors added a hands-on experience to formal book learning in ways that, more than 100 years later, still give University classes their distinctive immediacy.

Structural change also overtook the College in the postwar era. Not surprisingly, given the lawyerly nature of writing legislation, a revived law department, not seen since 1828, re-emerged in 1865. It was destined to stretch unbroken to its present-day embodiment—the National Law Center.

In the early 1870s, Congress, too, brought about changes. Acting at the trustees' request in 1871, it severed the College's Baptist ties (not quite forever, as it turned out) and, two years later, elevated the institution to the status of a university. The former it accomplished simply by altering the charter to provide for a non-denominational, self-perpetuating board of trustees.

*One of the many contemporary
drawings of the Lincoln death scene.*

JAMES CLARK WELLING

The new board promptly named James Clark Welling Columbian's first lay president; he became one of its most dynamic leaders ever. Welling not only showed considerable talent as a fundraiser; he also kept abreast of developments in higher education. Putting forward what he called "the university idea," he persuaded the trustees who, in turn, successfully petitioned Congress in 1873 to recharter Columbian College as Columbian University.

That same year, Welling—clearly as part of his effort to create a university in fact—secured a major endowment from William Corcoran, a long-time benefactor and co-founder of the Riggs National Bank. Thanks to Corcoran's generosity, Welling launched the lineal ancestor of today's School of Engineering and Applied Science. Founded in 1873 as the Corcoran Scientific School, the new unit was soon offering courses in surveying, civil engineering (construction), the science of machinery, and agricultural chemistry.

By the early eighties, Welling faced another challenge. While the professional schools had flourished, the war's devastation had perilously reduced the undergraduate population. Most of the students, who for 40 years had lived, studied, and romped on College Hill, had hailed from Dixie, where the student pool was yielding no more than a few dozen students, diminished by the South's sluggish economic recovery. Rather than let the undergraduate college go by the board, Welling decided it was time to relocate.

Piece by piece, between 1881 and 1884, he gathered all units of Columbian University into the downtown area, astutely placing them nearer to the bread and butter of the professional schools' population. To Welling it also made sense to sell off the College Hill property, now in a state of disrepair, and to use the proceeds to finance the new downtown building program. Resident students would have to fend for themselves. In fact, by 1881 only 39 students still living on College Hill had to look elsewhere for housing.

Welling's orchestration of the University's first relocation was soon complete. His plans called for a monumentally impressive structure that went up at H and 15th Streets. It opened for classes in October 1884, but despite its roominess—it was intended to accommodate classes for all but the medical students—the new University building soon posed room scheduling problems not unlike those administrators still face. Then, as now, time sharing offered a makeshift solution: daytime classes for undergraduates, evening classes for professional students.

The move downtown—or mid-town, as it was then—also meant taking advantage of new technology: on July 27, 1893, the trustees authorized the installation of the University's first telephone—in, as one might guess, the treasurer's office.

(Above) James Clarke Welling
served as Columbian's sixth
president and first lay leader,
1871-1894.

(Right) Medical school sophomore
class, 1911.

(Above) William Wilson Corcoran,
president of the Corporation
(now referred to as the Board of
Trustees), 1869-1888, was a principal benefactor of the University
in the late 19th century.

(Right) In the fall of 1888,
Mabel Nelson Thurston became
the first female undergraduate
admitted to GW.

WOMEN

Gender issues in the 1880s generated a number of "firsts" as well as a few dust-ups. Although Oberlin College had long since pioneered coeducation, Columbian University was slow to follow. On the down side, the law faculty in 1883 thought about it and then voted not to admit women, announcing dismissively that women attorneys were "not required by any public want."

The members of the medical faculty were somewhat more venturesome. In late 1884, they admitted four women, but soon found reason to regret it. Although Clara Bliss Hinds earned the University's first medical degree awarded to a woman in 1887, the faculty ultimately succumbed to the ambiguities of Victorian sensibility. After trying for seven years to maintain separate-sex medical instruction, the faculty reached the point where, they concluded, the "strain on modesty" had become too great.

While the professional schools dithered, Columbian College plunged in boldly. In the fall of 1888, its faculty voted to test the waters of coeducation by admitting Mabel Nelson Thurston, its first female undergraduate. From the ripples of that first test, a tidal wave of Columbian Women has since swept across the campus. Since 1986, women undergraduates have consistently outnumbered the men. Today, Thurston Hall, at the corner of F and 19th, commemorates her lonely breakthrough.

THE LATE 19TH CENTURY

On the academic front, the University also granted its first Ph.D. degrees in 1888, to two members of its own faculty. It institutionalized the award of this highest academic degree in 1893 when it opened one of the nation's first schools of graduate studies. Doctorates thereafter could be earned in science, medicine, and the liberal arts.

(Left) "The Original Thirteen" women to attend Columbian College.

(Above) The Class of 1899 graphically depicted.

In 1898, the Baptists had a last chance at stewardship when Congress—always freer with charter changes than hard cash—voted to let them take over the Board of Trustees. The prevailing hope at the time rested on the assumption that, if the University were returned to Baptist stewardship, a sense of denominational pride would loosen their purse strings and put the institution on a firm financial footing. The hope quickly proved illusory. When the purse strings stayed tied, Congress in 1904 backtracked, restoring the University—then and for all time—to nonsectarian status. In the same stroke, while retaining the designation Columbian for our arts and sciences college, it gave us the name we still live by: The George Washington University.

Four years later, as if to announce its arrival in the big time, the GW football team won the South Atlantic championship, an event matched in significance, perhaps, by the trustees' decision that year to drop Latin from the B.A. requirements.

Returning to 1898, the year of the war with Spain, alumni would later recall proudly that among the University's volunteers for wartime service was a Columbian College junior named William L. Mitchell. GW's first nationally famous graduate, a wartime drop-out, Mitchell came back (after another war) to complete his B.A. in 1919 and to receive it, "as of the class of 1899." A decade-and-a-half later, the nation would come to know him as General "Billy" Mitchell, the controversial advocate of air power. GW still remembers him in a residence hall named in his honor.

Backdating degrees, we might note, would become something of a GW tradition. In 1936, the University belatedly awarded an academic degree to John Foster Dulles who, impatient with residency requirements, had dropped out of the law school in 1911 rather than complete his third year.

(Above) Charles William Needham, the University's "enterprising" eighth president, 1902-1910.

(Left) Abram Lisner, a University benefactor and trustee, was a prominent merchant.

(Below) The Masonic Temple, 13th and H Streets, and New York Avenue. The law school used the upper two floors from 1910-1921.

FINANCIAL CRISIS

The University's brief fling with the Baptists once more spotlighted its most persistent problem: finances. Worse was to come. In 1910, the University nearly went bankrupt. Plagued by managerial incompetence, hit by economic recession, but most of all, the victim of too much expansion with too few resources, GW barely stayed afloat, its decks awash with mortgages, unpaid bills, and annual deficits, buoyed only by President Charles Needham's indomitable optimism for gifts and grants that never materialized. As University Historian Elmer Kayser writes sardonically: "Needham warned his board about incurring debts, but kept on spending."

Amid trustee resignations, the crisis took an ugly turn. As Kayser delicately puts it, the University suffered an "impairment of endowment funds." In fact, the "impairment" smacked more of a gross mishandling of University monies, a conclusion the U.S. Attorney General reached when his office formally investigated. The principal culprit was President Needham or, perhaps more accurately, Needham's grandiose enterprises. In an effort to pay for his costly projects, the president had illicitly dipped into endowment funds. The short-term consequences were severe. Forced by the Attorney General's office to restore the endowment, the University, in turn, was forced to sell off its major downtown properties. Suffice it to note that today no University building bears the name of Charles Needham.

Suddenly beset with a calamitous cash flow, the University seemed to explode across the Washington cityscape. The medical school and hospital remained intact, but the law faculty had to take refuge in the top floors of the Masonic Temple, where they lodged uncomfortably for more than a decade. Meanwhile, the undergraduates of the "college" met for classes in rented row-houses along Eye Street. Yet, in what passed for its dark ages, the University never missed a class. Instruction continued unbroken.

Survival ensured, recovery came slowly. Budget cuts helped. So did tuition hikes (raised to $150 a year). But more than anything else, the University owed its recovery to a scholarly admiral named Charles Stockton who, through sheer determination and stern insistence on budget balancing, put the University back together again. The admiral/president wielded a sharp budget axe and, remarkably, kept his promises not to let expenses exceed income. Stockton Hall is his fitting memorial.

THE NEW LOCALE

In 1912, a loan from Riggs Bank enabled the University to purchase a building at 2023 G Street. Here for a time GW housed all of its arts and sciences departments.

As the financial crisis receded in the years just prior to World War I, the trustees managed to buy additional parcels of land and

Delegates to the inauguration of University President William Mather Lewis (right) photographed at the White House, 1923, with President Calvin Coolidge (center). Chief Justice William Howard Taft (left) was the delegate of Yale University.

buildings in the G Street area. In 1919, trustee and prominent merchant Abram Lisner, in an act of timely benevolence that would not be his last, gave $24,500 to pay off all the mortgages on the G Street properties.

The second relocation began to take shape, and while finances may have been low, student spirit remained high. The year Woodrow Wilson was re-elected, a recently organized Student Council breathed new life into a moribund intercollegiate athletics program.

During the war, classes met without interruption and, like wartime classes at other universities, responded to the perceived need to add military training to traditional education. In 1917, GW mustered a company of Coast Artillery whose members, far from defending coastal America, saw action in the Meuse-Argonne offensive. A minor interruption did occur in the spring of 1918, when at the

The Hall of Government building on the corner of 21st and G Streets was completed in 1938.

height of the flu epidemic, the University suspended classes for four weeks. Graduation was late that year, and a half century would pass before classes were again suspended, then under the quite different circumstances of student unrest.

The 1920s were a time of measured growth. In the year 1924 alone, Corcoran and Stockton Halls were completed and cornerstoned, respectively. Honoring the 19th-century benefactor whose name had once decorated the Corcoran Scientific School, Corcoran Hall became the first new structure to be built in the University's present location. In the "scientific" tradition of its namesake once removed, Corcoran still houses the chemistry and physics departments. Across the University Yard that year the law school's permanent home, Stockton Hall, began to rise on its foundations.

While classrooms and offices took top priority for the University's expanding programs, the construction of dormitories, now known as residence halls, came at a slower pace. Ironically, or perhaps fittingly, the first beneficiaries of on-campus housing were the women. Admitted to the liberal arts in 1888, but long spurned by the law faculty and only briefly admitted to medical training, GW women had broken through into the professional schools only as recently as 1913. Now, in the late '30s, they not only found a place in classrooms, they also had a place to live. Thanks to a $200,000 gift from Hattie M. Strong, at least some of the women were now spared the long streetcar rides or their alternative, the rooming houses nearby. For men, the choice would remain the streetcar, the rooming house, or a fraternity house.

THE CONCRETE CAMPUS

Despite these improvements, the University was not physically prepossessing. One veteran of World War II, who came to study at GW in 1946, said that it took him a long time to find the campus: "It seemed to be situated among a bunch of row houses, grocery stores, streetcar lines, and automobile traffic; it had a postage stamp-size campus." Undergraduates who arrived in 1958 received a handbook that began with these words, "Well here you are at GW and you're probably wondering: What campus? True, we keep it carefully camouflaged, but it's here—the only concrete campus in captivity."

The concrete campus had its share of attractions and charms. To be sure, it occupied a decidedly urban terrain, with none of the open fields and gothic quadrangles that marked other universities. Instead, much of the University was contained within a square city block, bounded by G, H, 20th, and 21st Streets in the Foggy Bottom section of Northwest Washington. In 1934, the University authorized the construction of Lisner Hall. By 1939, with architects working in a depression idiom that included used bricks, movable interior walls, and exposed piping and wiring, a complete row of buildings along G Street, including what are today Bell, Stuart, and Lisner Halls, stood ready for occupancy. This group of utilitarian, multi-purpose buildings joined such other structures as the Hall of Government (G and 21st Streets) and the "Tin Tabernacle" to form a campus.

(Above) Students enjoy some rest and relaxation on the "roof garden" of Hattie M. Strong Residence Hall for Women, southwest corner of 21st and G Streets, Circa 1938.

(Left) In earlier days, students sketch in GW Prof. Richard Lahey's art class at the Corcoran.

THE "TIN TABERNACLE"

Nothing symbolized the sorry state of GW's physical plant better than the "Tin Tabernacle." It was a makeshift field house, built in 1924 of temporary materials. Almost immediately GW administrators and students talked of replacing it, yet it lasted into the 1970s. It contained training facilities best described as marginal. For example, students who took gym in the Tabernacle competed for the use of the seven showers at the end of the class. The entire facility held 11 showers, but four were reserved for varsity athletes. During the season when basketball and football overlapped, 75 football players and 20 basketball players did their best to cope with those facilities.

When the basketball players practiced in the Tabernacle, they used a court that had only three feet of space between the court boundaries and the wall. Playing intercollegiate games in the Tabernacle quickly became out of the question, since the facility seated only about 70 people. Even as a site for physical education, the Tabernacle had its shortcomings. A class could undertake only one activity at a time. It was impossible, for example, to run a half court basketball game and a volleyball game simultaneously. The dimensions of the facility were only 140 by 60 feet.

Women, for the most part, took their gym classes in other parts of the city. Often they traveled to the YWCA, half a mile from campus, and still they were expected to return in time for class in the next hour. The women swam at the Y, since GW had no pool of its own, played tennis on the State Department courts, and hiked to the Ellipse for soccer and hockey. This situation persisted until 1960, when the University purchased what became the women's gymnasium on 23rd Street.

Ventilation in the Tabernacle was so poor that windows in the dressing room had to be left open. Campus visitors were often shocked to look into the window and see a bunch of half-dressed men. Lighting was dim enough that physical recreation often involved the threat of physical injury. It was, all in all, less than an ideal facility. In 1952, *The Hatchet* described it as "miserable by all accounts."

(Left) The gymnasium, "The Tin Tabernacle," on the south side of H Street west of 20th, served as the campus's field house from 1924 into the 1970s.

(Right) The 1908 football team—South Atlantic Champions—was one of the University's most winning athletic teams in GW's history.

(Below) Women's field hockey team, 1925.

(Left) In 1942, students head to a GW game.

(Top) Faculty Follies, 1948, featuring (sitting l-r) Roderic Davison, Lawrence Daniel Folkemer, Charles Keating, and (standing) Howard Merrifield.

WASHINGTON AND TRADITIONAL COLLEGE LIFE

GW students endured the Tin Tabernacle and even grew to be nostalgic about it. Part of the attraction of GW's mundane edifices derived from their location in Washington, D.C. Students who came to GW did so at least in part because they were attracted to the city. When they arrived, they learned, as the Class of 1958 did, of how the campus branched out "into the city—to the medical school downtown, the Corcoran Gallery where University art courses are taught, the Pentagon where classes in nuclear physics are taught, and Frog Island, the football practice field across Memorial Bridge on the banks of the historic Potomac River. All the facilities of the nation's capital are at your immediate disposal—government agency pamphlets; the Library of Congress, which supplements the University's big library; Griffith Stadium, GW's home stadium."

Yet, for all of the constraints of a cramped campus and for all of the opportunities provided by the University's location, the remarkable thing was the way in which The George Washington

BUY WAR STAMPS

(Top left) Ice skaters from the women's athletics department salute their audience after performing a precision number in the 1940s.

(Below) A slice of college life in the '40s: A room in Staughton Hall dormitory for women, 1946.

(Bottom left) Students sold war stamps during World War II.

(Above) Homecoming "Rally Before the Rally," 1940s.

(Right) Sorority and fraternity dances and other events marked the social nature of the time.

(Bottom) Gloria Klapp, Homecoming Queen, and Bob Flanders, student co-chairman of Homecoming, November 1946.

(Left) With the help of the G.I. Bill, World War II veterans signed up for a GW education.

(Right) GW alumnae Lt. (j.g.) Jean O. Casanova and Lt. Catherine D. Callahan were WAVES attached to the Legislative Division of the Navy Judge Advocate General's Office.

University students faithfully re-enacted the traditional rituals of campus life. As early as 1919, even before the move to the Foggy Bottom campus was completed, GW's 4,280 students each paid a fee of $10. In return, the students received subscriptions to *The Hatchet*, then and now the campus newspaper, and *The Cherry Tree*, the school yearbook, as well as admission to all student contests and approved student activities. The fee even paid for free medical and hospital treatment.

The 1930s marked the height of what might be called traditional college life at George Washington. Fifteen fraternities and 12 sororities dominated the social scene. The ritual of homecoming began in 1932, with a football game played against the University of Oklahoma. By 1941, homecoming had become established to the extent that pictures of the Homecoming Queen appeared in *The Washington Star*. Every year fraternities competed to have the best-decorated house, and the entire campus participated in the election of the Campus Sweetheart. Homecoming culminated in an all-University dance. Commencement followed a similar time-honored pattern. The week of graduation featured a dinner, prom, baccalaureate, and class night exercises. The annual social calendar was marked by four Buff and Blue Dances.

VETERANS

These campus traditions persisted throughout the 1940s and 1950s. For those who lived in wartime Washington, it must have seemed as though everyone not on active duty had camped on their doorstep. Some came to teach, some came to learn, all came to do their part in the war effort. GW did its share. Under contract to the U.S. Office of Education, the University over a four-year period offered 387 courses, mostly in engineering, science, and "war training," to some 13,000 students. Meanwhile, far from their old classrooms, an estimated 7,000 GW graduates saw active service in the armed forces.

Just as the Marshall Plan spared the economy a serious postwar depression, so did the G.I. Bill boost GW enrollments—thrusting the University into an unparalleled postwar expansion. Not known,

until an article appeared recently in *Smithsonian* magazine, was that *Hatchet* editor Don Balfour was the first ex-G.I. to sign up. The day after President Franklin D. Roosevelt signed Public Law 346, ex-Corporal Balfour, a Washington native who had been paying his own way at GW, turned up at the office of the VA's vocational officer looking for a news story. After hearing the benefits explained, Balfour asked if he could sign up. "Certainly" was the answer, and even though the VA hadn't yet printed the forms, Balfour on June 23, 1944, led the parade of millions into what proved to be America's soundest investment in human resources.

Even as the arrival of veterans began to alter the rhythms of University life in 1945 and 1946, GW students found time to hold the Haba Hop, described as an informal skirt and sweater affair, and to precede it with a Tug of War between sorority and fraternity members. In this period, the University's hospital was still at 13th and H. Guests and parents stayed at the Roger Smith Hotel on Pennsylvania Avenue and 18th Street. At the corner of 20th and G Streets was Maxwell Cafeteria, whose owners declared themselves "caterers to the campus."

If nothing else, the presence of veterans in the late 1940s and early 1950s swelled the size of the University and put even more pressure on its less-than-adequate physical plant. During the academic year that began in 1946, 7,000 veterans registered for classes, using the financial benefits provided by the G.I. Bill. That summer enrollment for the first summer session reached a peak of 6,027—3,940 of the enrollees were veterans, eager to catch up on their course requirements. In a short time, the University opened an Office of Veterans' Education that attended to the housing, employment, and counseling needs of the students who had served in World War II.

The veterans, more mature than the typical undergraduates, increased the caliber of scholarship at George Washington. Calvin Linton was an English professor who later became dean of the Columbian College. When he retired in 1984, he remembered the students of this era as the best he had ever taught. Among those whom Linton undoubtedly instructed was Elliot Liebow, fresh out of the Marines. Studying with Linton and his colleagues, Liebow earned a master's degree in English. He made his mark as an anthropologist, writing the award-winning *Tally's Corner: A Study of Negro Streetcorner Men*. Later, he headed a center at the National Institute of Mental Health where he studied contemporary issues such as women on welfare in strikingly original ways. GW, in the period of ferment after the war, launched Liebow, among many others, on a career that would influence the shape of intellectual discussion in the postwar era.

The New York Times

"All the News That's Fit to Print"

Copyright, 1954, by The New York Times Company.

NEW YORK, TUESDAY, MAY 18, 1954.

VOL. CIII...No. 35,178.

Entered as Second-Class Matter.
Post Office, New York, N. Y.

HIGH COURT BANS SCHOOL

9-TO-0 DECISION GRANTS T

McCarthy Hearing Off a Week as Eise

SENATOR IS IRATE

President Orders Aides Not to Disclose Details of Top-Level Meeting

President's letter and excerpts from transcript, Pages 24, 25, 26.

By W. H. LAWRENCE
Special to The New York Times.

WASHINGTON, May 17—A secrecy directive by President Eisenhower resulted today in an abrupt recess for at least a week of the Senate's Army-McCarthy hearings.

Democratic and Republican Senators, some publicly and some privately, predicted that the investigation might never resume in earnest. However, there were other Senators who insisted that the investigation would go on to completion.

The recess was voted after Herbert Brownell Jr., the Attorney General, disclosed formally that criminal prosecutions might be instituted against those involved in the "preparation and dissemination" of an altered, condensed but still confidential Federal Bureau of Investigation report. This was offered in evidence last week by Senator Jo-

Communist Arms Unloaded in Guatemala By Vessel From Polish Port, U. S. Learns

State Department Views News Gravely Because of Red Infiltration

Special to The New York Times.

WASHINGTON, May 17—The State Department said today that it had reliable information that "an important shipment of arms" had been sent from Communist-controlled territory to Guatemala.

It said the arms, now being unloaded at Puerto Barrios, Guatemala, had been shipped from Stettin, a former German Baltic seaport, which has been occupied by Communist Poland since World War II. The Guatemalan regime has been frequently accused of being influenced by Communists.

"Because of the origin of these arms, the point of their embarkation, their destination and the quantity of arms involved, the Department of State considers that this is a development of gravity," the announcement said.

A freighter arrived at Puerto

The New York Times   May 18, 1954
Site of arms arrival (cross)

Embassy Says Nation of Central America May Buy Munitions Anywhere

Barrios last Saturday, the State Department reported, carrying a large shipment of armament consigned to the Guatemalan Government.

The State Department did not divulge the exact quantity of the arms, their nature or where they had been manufactured.

Reliable sources told The New York Times, however, that ten freight car loads of goods listed in the manifest as "hardware" had been unloaded from this ship and sent to the city of Guatemala since Sunday. Guatemala is 150 miles from Puerto Barrios. The

Continued on Page 10. Column 5

REACTION OF SOUTH

'Breathing Spell' for Adjustment Tempers Region's Feelings

By JOHN N. POPHAM
Special to The New York Times.

CHATTANOOGA, Tenn., May 17—The South's reaction to the Supreme Court's decision outlawing racial segregation in public schools appeared to be tempered considerably today.

The time lag allowed for carrying out the required transition seemed to be the major factor in that reaction.

Southern leaders of both races in political, educational and community service fields expressed comment that covered a wide range. Some spoke bitter words that verged on defiance. Others ranged from sharp disagreement to predictions of peaceful, successful adjustment in accord with the ruling.

But underneath the surface much of the comment, it was evident that many Southerners recognized that the decision was handed down the legal principle rejecting segregation in public education facilities.

They also noted that it would open a challenge to the [...] to join in working out a p[...] of necessary changes in the [...] ent bi-racial school system[...]

Three of the most illu[...] viewpoints were those of [...]

SOVIET BIDS VIENNA CEASE 'INTRIGUES'

Envoy Warns Austrian Chief on Inciting East Zone—Raab Denies Charges

City Colleges' Board Can't Pick Chairman

The Board of Higher Education was unable to elect a chairman at its annual meeting last night at Hunter College.

A spokesman said it was the first time "within memory of board officials" that such a situation had occurred.

Nineteen of the twenty-one

2 TAX PROJECTS DIE IN ESTIMATE BOARD

Beer Levy and More Parking Collections Killed—Payroll Impost Still Weighed

CHARLES G. BENNETT

The Quiet Campus

LATE CITY EDITION

Fair and cool today. Mostly sunny, continued cool tomorrow.

Temperature Range Today—Max., 68; Min., 52
Temperatures Yesterday—Max., 69; Min., 61

Full U. S. Weather Bureau Report, Page 51

mes.

Times Square, New York 36, N. Y.
Telephone LAckawanna 4-1000

FIVE CENTS

EGREGATION;
ME TO COMPLY

nhower Bars Report

1896 RULING UPSET

'Separate but Equal'
Doctrine Held Out of
Place in Education

*Text of Supreme Court decision
is printed on Page 15.*

By LUTHER A. HUSTON
Special to The New York Times.

WASHINGTON, May 17—The Supreme Court unanimously outlawed today racial segregation in public schools.

Chief Justice Earl Warren read two opinions that put the stamp of unconstitutionality on school systems in twenty-one states and the District of Columbia where segregation is permissive or mandatory.

The court, taking cognizance of the problems involved in the integration of the school systems concerned, put over until the next term, beginning in October, the formulation of decrees to effectuate its 9-to-0 decision.

The opinions set aside the "separate but equal" doctrine laid down by the Supreme Court in 1896.

"In the field of public education," Chief Justice Warren said, "the doctrine of 'separate but equal' has no place. Separate educational facilities are inherently unequal."

He stated the question and supplied the answer as follows:

"We come then to the question presented: Does segregation of children in public schools solely on the basis of race, even though

EQUAL JUSTICE UNDER

Associated Press Wirephoto

LEADERS IN SEGREGATION FIGHT: Lawyers who led battle before U. S. Supreme Court for abolition of segregation in public schools congratulate one another as they leave court after announcement of decision. Left to right: George E. C. Hayes, Thurgood Marshall and James M. Nabrit.

MORETTIS' LAWYER
MUST BARE TALKS

RULING TO FIGURE
IN '54 CAMPAIGN

THE 1950S

Despite the presence on campus of veterans of both World War II and the Korean conflict, the 1950s were not marked by a new sensibility among the members of the student body. Instead, this decade of economic growth and subterranean intellectual revolt reinforced past patterns. Elaborate festivities remained a permanent feature of undergraduate life. The 1957 homecoming celebration was typical of its time. It took "GWU in 2002" as its theme and included a pep rally that featured the presentation of the football squads and the unmasking of "George" and "Martha."

Each year a male and female student volunteered to play the roles of George and Martha Washington. They patrolled the sidelines of the football games as University mascots; their faces were carefully concealed behind masks. Their names remained a well-kept secret until homecoming.

After the unmasking came the selection of the five Homecoming Queen finalists, known as the Colonial beauties, who made their appearance on the Lisner stage escorted by ROTC cadets. That served as the finale of what a student publication described as "the most colorful display of enthusiasm in George Washington annals."

Other times of the year also held their special rituals during this decade. In winter, a Christmas tree lighting ceremony took place on Lisner terrace overlooking the Yard. After the University president lit the tree, the assembled students and faculty listened to the traditional Christmas story and sang carols with the Traveling Troubadours, GW's itinerant glee club.

Each year also featured the Goat Show in which new sorority pledges prepared comic skits that were performed in Lisner Auditorium. They competed for a large cup that was presented to the cleverest, most original, best presented, and most appealing performance.

In the spring, students took a Colonial cruise down the Potomac to Marshall Hall, a popular amusement park. The University provided two boats home. One left at five o'clock, but the second departed late in the evening and became a romantic moonlight cruise, complete with dancing on deck.

In this era, students often stopped to eat at Bassin's GW Inn, located at 1920 Pennsylvania Avenue, which, in good American style, featured kosher corned beef, pastrami, pizza, chili, and spaghetti. It was open 24 hours a day. Slightly more upscale was the Varsity Inn at 20th and G.

SOCIAL SETTINGS

Despite the presence of fraternities and sororities in these years, GW students continually complained of a lack of social amenities on the Foggy Bottom campus. In 1935, a partial solution arrived in the

(Left) Jitterbug contest winners Alice Dunn and Gordon Fisher at the Jazz Concert, held at the Bayou, during Winter Weekend 1957. Such events were common during this decade.

(Right) Members of the University's growing volunteer pep band try out a few notes for well-known band leader Benny Goodman, 1954.

(Below) Caroling at the Christmas tree lighting, December 12, 1955.

*Students kick back in the Student
Union Annex, circa 1955.*

form of the Student Club, located in the basement of Bell Hall. Open from 8:30 in the morning until 7:00 in the evening, it provided a place for between-class gatherings. A piano and juke box added to the enjoyment of the informal atmosphere. The club had room for about 200 people, among whom were always to be found at least four playing bridge. The club served snacks and sold school supplies in a noisy, slightly raucous atmosphere. Freshmen were warned not to attempt to study there "unless you have phenomenal powers of concentration."

In 1949, the Student Union building opened at 2125 G Street, next to the firehouse. Compared with the Student Club, it was a more elaborate and better equipped place, with a first-floor cafeteria that served breakfast, lunch, and dinner. A second-floor social lounge contained radios and comfortable chairs and sofas, and a fourth-floor recreation room had a radio and record players for student use. The Student Union soon became the heart of the campus.

Margaret Truman often found herself hounded for pictures by roving newspaper photographers.

As a student hangout, the Student Union competed only with Quigley's. When students reminisced about their undergraduate life at GW, they invariably mentioned getting a coke at Quigley's. As one student who attended GW during the war years put it, "Quigley's corner drug store supplied us with snacks, blue books, and No-Doz pills for exam week." Another described the store as the "pivot of GW life." Quigley's occupied such a prominent position in GW lore that in 1971 when the "Voice of America" made a program on the 150th anniversary of GW, it decided to call the program, "The View from Quigley's." In the program, the place was described as the perennial corner store and as the unifying thread of GW.

Even in the face of tremendous changes, Quigley's lasted as a GW institution. When Hillary Rodham Clinton addressed GW graduates at the 1994 Commencement, she recalled her days in Washington as a student intern and mentioned stopping in at Quigley's. But the store fell upon hard times in the 1970s, and in 1974 the University bought the property that housed the store. By that time, Quigley's was reduced, in one student's words, to becoming "a place to have ice cream between classes." Another student complained that "it looks like a dump. The only thing I go in there to buy is Life Savers." Eventually Quigley's closed, and the site on the corner of 21st and G Streets became the home of the geography department. Preservationists rightly insisted, however, the the location be permanently marked as the home of Quigley's.

LIVING HISTORY AT GW

Quigley's, like almost everything else at George Washington, was more than a student hangout. One could go there and at any particular time observe a piece of history. Students in the mid-1940s might discover Margaret Truman, the campus's most famous student, waiting for her father to meet her for a soda. Indeed, Margaret Truman was a campus celebrity; she found herself hounded for pictures by roving photographers from the city's five daily newspapers. When she would graciously oblige, they would often pose her seated in the smokey basement setting of the Student Club with, in one student's words, "the ugly pipes overhead and those awful wooden tables with everyone's initials carved in them."

When Margaret Truman received her bachelor's degree from George Washington in 1946, the president of the United States presented her with her diploma. Then, minutes later, President Truman, like Warren Harding, Herbert Hoover, and Calvin Coolidge before him, received a GW honorary degree.

Encounters with history at GW could also be very informal. In the spring of 1947, two female undergraduates decided to take some time off between exams and walk to the Jefferson Memorial. On their way, they noticed an official limousine that drew up and stopped. Inside were Dwight D. Eisenhower and the famous British

(Above) At the 1946
Commencement, President Harry
S Truman accepted an honorary
GW degree and Margaret Truman
received her bachelor's degree.
They are shown here with GW
President Cloyd Heck Marvin
(left).

(Right) Students browse in the
cooperative store, June 1958.

Army Commander, Bernard L. Montgomery (complete with beret), who paused long enough to stand up and give the women a snappy salute. "Like two little boys with their hands caught in the cookie jar, the two World War II heroes drove off, grinning from ear to ear," one of the women recalled.

ATHLETIC GLORY

Besides these opportunities to glimpse history, the campus also gained a sense of unity from GW's participation in intercollegiate athletics. In the 1930s, the University fielded a more-than-respectable football squad that competed against some of the major teams in the nation. In 1934, the Buff and Blue, as they were known, compiled a 6-3-1 record in football. That year was one of three in which Alphonse "Tuffy" Leemans, the greatest football player in GW history, set rushing records. Opponents included Vanderbilt and Oklahoma, and home games were played at Griffith Stadium, a field on which the Senators baseball team and later the Redskins football team competed. Up to 25,000 people showed up for the games.

In 1936, the team won seven of nine games, the best showing in GW history. In the final game of the season, against West Virginia, GW eeked out a 7-2 victory when the team scored a touchdown with only four minutes left to play. Also that year, the team was behind 12-7 on the Wake Forest 11-yard line with two seconds left. A touchdown pass in the last second gave GW the victory.

If the University made a respectable showing in football, it excelled at basketball. After a 2-8 season during the winter of 1928-29, the University did not have another losing year until 1956-7. In 1935, a legend began when Bill Reinhart made his coaching debut. He coached for 24 of the next 29 years. In the 1935 season, GW went 16-3. Then, in 1936, Bob Farris, later athletic director of GW, arrived and proceeded to exhibit All-American form. In 1942, Reinhart left GW to serve in the Navy, having compiled a record of 100 wins and fewer than 40 losses. After the war, he picked up where he had left off. In 1955-56, the team, led by Corky Devlin and Joe Holup, went 19-7.

GW's basketball program produced one of the University's most famous alumni—one whose GW tenure also was interrupted by World War II. Arnold "Red" Auerbach, Class of 1940, left GW for a stint in the Navy and then began his professional coaching career in 1946-1947. After four years with the Washington Capitols, he moved to the Boston Celtics. In Boston, Auerbach became one of the most celebrated coaches in the history of professional sports. He won an unequalled 11 championships with the Celtics, including

Alphonse "Tuffy" Leemans, the greatest football player in GW history, looks for daylight on a kick return in the Alabama game, 1934.

9 straight. In 1967, he became the club's general manager, maintaining the Celtics as perennial title contenders. Even though he is now president and chief executive officer of the Celtics, Auerbach keeps his residence in Washington and remains very interested in GW athletics.

THE PERNICIOUS PATTERN OF SEGREGATION

When Auerbach played basketball for GW, the team, like the University itself and like the audiences that watched sporting contests, was limited to whites. This pernicious pattern underscored the fact that, as GW students benefited from their Washington location, they also shared a sense of frustration over the city's inability

The GW football team played its home games at Griffith Stadium until the 1960s.

to solve fundamental problems. Segregation was undoubtedly among the most serious of those problems. The issue, at GW and in the city itself, came to a head in the postwar era.

One celebrated incident involved the first commercial production ever held at Lisner Auditorium. The facility was among the most impressive auditoriums in the city. It could then seat 1,550, and it contained ultra-modern light and sound systems as well as a huge 59-foot stage, said to be the largest south of New York City. It was only natural that theater producers would seek out Lisner as a site for their major productions.

To inaugurate Lisner as a commercial theater, the University agreed to host a Broadway-bound presentation of "Joan of Lorraine," starring 29-year-old Ingrid Bergman. With the play set to open on

Continued on p. 62

The School of Engineering and Applied Science

Organized on October 1, 1884, as the Corcoran Scientific School of Columbian University, the school, situated in the University Building at 15th and H Streets, offered evening courses in science and technology. These led to the degrees of Bachelor of Science, Civil Engineer, Mechanical Engineer, and Mining Engineer. Although the school lacked the national distinction that was to come, it was among the first to accept women for degree candidacy in engineering.

GETTING ORGANIZED

As was characteristic of so many of GW's endeavors, the school changed names and locations in the early years of its existence. In 1903, for example, the Corcoran Scientific School, the School of Graduate Studies, and the Columbian College were merged into a single Department of Arts and Sciences. This department offered graduate engineering degrees. Administrative changes led to the creation of the Washington College of Engineering in 1905. One of several semi-independent undergraduate colleges of the University, it granted undergraduate degrees in engineering and architecture.

In 1909, this college changed its name to the College of Engineering and Mechanic Arts. The curriculum emphasized the acquisition of both theoretical and practical knowledge. By emphasizing

theory over what might be called technology, the school gained a distinctive identity among the nation's engineering schools.

This emphasis remained, even as the title of the school kept on changing: to the College of Engineering in 1914 and still later to the School of Engineering. In 1962, the name of the school became the School of Engineering and Applied Science.

ENGINEERING IN THE NATION'S SERVICE

The School of Engineering and Applied Science's history has been marked by distinguished service to the nation. In 1940, with the nation on the edge of

The School of Engineering and Applied Science started in 1884 as the Corcoran Scientific School of Columbian University. Just prior to World War II, the school created seven special courses to prepare the country for the stresses that war would put on America's productive capacity.

war, the school created seven special courses to prepare the country for the stresses that war would put on America's productive capacity. Topics included concrete testing and map making. By 1944, these courses had evolved into 15-week war-training courses in such topics as the elements of interior ballistics.

In 1954, the school inaugurated a program for the degree of Master of Engineering Administration, intended to serve executives in both industry and government who ran complex and technologically demanding programs. During the next year, the University laid the cornerstone for Tompkins Hall, which became the new headquarters for the engineering school, even though various projects continued to be housed throughout the Foggy Bottom neighborhood (even today key parts of the school are housed in the Academic Center).

On June 20, 1956, a vault for the "future in the year 2056" was dedicated in Tompkins Hall. It contained engineering and other tools that were typical in 1956, such as a slide rule—an instrument that engineers and other technically minded students wore like a badge of honor until the dawn of the computer age.

"Although we are housed in a modern 1956 building," wrote one leader of the school in 1960, "the equipment facilities of the school are minimal for the educational effort we undertake. As a consequence instruction tends to be somewhat more theoretical than some consider to be optimum for professional study." Yet, working within these constraints, the school continued to develop new and creative endeavors, often in partnership with government and industry.

If the school had a breakthrough year, it might have been 1968—when Harold Liebowitz was appointed dean. Liebowitz helped to transform the school from what might be described as a night school for part-time students into a full-fledged institution for the study of engineering.

THE LOGISTICS RESEARCH PROJECT

Soon after Harold Liebowitz arrived, Bill Marlow brought the Logistics Research Project into the engineering school. This project had begun long before, in 1951, to explore possible uses of scientific methods and automatic computers for logistics planning in the Navy. The sorts of problems that the project considered included how to determine how many men were needed for a particular military operation and what sorts of supplies they might require. The project also did research relevant to such things as figuring out how many supply parts a submarine should carry and how to face other, similar logistical challenges.

Marlow was trained in mathematics, and his work involved the use of sophisticated mathematical techniques such as non-linear programming. In time, GW became and remained a leader in Marlow's field, known as operations research.

Although Marlow insisted that the work from his project be published in non-classified journals, the project nonetheless proceeded in relative secrecy under high security. At one time in the 1950s, an armed guard scrutinized all those who entered the offices at 707 22nd Street. Marlow was always afraid that "somebody was going to get shot because some of the guards would be

(Left) Tompkins Hall of Engineering opened its doors in 1956.

(Above) GW acquired the FLAC-II computer from the Air Force in 1960. The Department of Electrical Engineering operated the FLAC-II for biomedical research. Nelson T. Grisamore, executive officer of the department, watches Thomas Wiggins install the computer.

(Right) Testing a Slender Column in the School of Engineering.

messing with those guns." He added, "As an ex-Navy officer, I was kind of horrified by it, but there was not much I could do."

The work involved the use of the most up-to-date computers. In 1951, ABEL became one of the first computers installed on the GW campus when it arrived in Staughton Hall for the use of the Logistics Research Project. In the manner of the era, it was a huge machine. With its air conditioning system, it occupied a large room, even though it lacked the computing power of an ordinary modern desktop computer. In the back of the machine, there were exposed telephone relays with open circuits, which created an acute sense of danger. Just to walk in back of the machine, Marlow recalled, one exposed one's self to grave harm.

The Logistics Research Project brought millions of dollars to GW and added to the University's reputation as a major research center. For all of that, it eventually ran into strong opposition because of its military sponsorship. Ironically, Marlow's work had long been declassified, yet the association with the military continued to attract deep suspicion. One day, for example, Marlow read a *Hatchet* headline that read, "Navy Logistics Works on Skyhawk Bombers." He recognized the headline as a dramatic form of overstatement; all that he and his co-workers were doing was taking data from the usage of repair parts and tying those data to the number of flying hours for airplanes. Marlow saw his work as solving an abstract problem in operations research; campus critics saw the work as helping to build the nation's war machine.

In 1969, responding to the intense criticism of the Vietnam War, the University decided to end its association with non-departmental projects sponsored by the military. Dean Liebowitz, who had himself worked for the Office of Naval Research, came to Marlow's rescue. He saw the project as one that was both lucrative and educationally valuable. "Do you want to go off and set up a think tank or do you want to stay?" he asked Marlow.

Marlow opted to stay. His program became part of the engineering administration and operations research department in the school of engineering. In time, operations research split off to form its own department. It remained a center of creative thought and endeavor, and its faculty included some of the most distinguished and most published members of the University.

In fields such as non-linear programming, GW ranked near the top in the nation. Professors Anthony Fiacco and Garth McCormick did outstanding work in the field of optimization. In 1981, Professor Nozer D. Singpurwalla started the Institute of Reliability and Risk Analysis to serve as a base for his research in the field of reliability. Among those organizations with whom he consulted were the Army Research Office, the Office of Naval Research, the National Science Foundation, and the Los Alamos National Laboratory. Don Gross, another member of the department, wrote one of the standard texts on "cuing" theory, which, although it involved complicated mathematics, dealt with a problem with which nearly everyone contends: determining the amount of time one will have to wait by observing the length of the line.

(Left) In 1971, the engineering school joined efforts with NASA's Langley Research Center to create the Joint Institute for Advancement of Flight Sciences. The school also started a similar program at Goddard Space Flight Center, concentrating on the areas of spacecraft and satellite design.

(Right) School of Engineering and Applied Science Professor Jack Harrald and his graduate students conduct research into disaster management—how well people respond to catastrophe. Shown are (left-right) Shyuan Cho, Michel Abchee, Harrald, Babak Fouladi, and Vinod Bagal.

(Below) Vice President Dan Quayle gave a congratulatory talk in the Smith Center on Aug. 17, 1991, to some 600 high school students completing GW's summer Science and Engineering Apprentice Program.

EDUCATIONAL AND RESEARCH ENDEAVORS

In 1969, the same year that Bill Marlow came to the engineering school, the University established the Continuing Engineering Education Program (CEEP). It became one of the most successful of such programs in the world, offering over 350 courses on six continents. Internationally renowned instructors, such as management guru Peter Drucker and efficiency expert W. Edwards Deming, served as instructors. In 1988, CEEP was one of the first programs of its type to offer management courses via satellite throughout both North and South America, in addition to providing a full range of books and videotapes for short courses.

Perhaps the most prominent of the engineering school's external programs began in 1971. In that year, the National Aeronautics and Space Administration's Langley Research Center joined with GW's School of Engineering and Applied Science to create the Joint Institute for Advancement of Flight Sciences. Through the Institute, the school did acclaimed work in acoustics, flight sciences, and computer-aided structural design. Three years earlier, the school had begun a residential, advanced-degree program at the NASA-Langley Research Center. By 1971, enrollment in this program had reached 150. By now the program has awarded over 700 graduate degrees and produced about 1,000 research presentations/publications.

Several years after starting the program at Langley, the school began a somewhat similar program at Goddard Space Flight Center. Professor Doug Jones, a longtime veteran of the school,

Sunforce I, GW's solar-powered automobile, in 1993 paraded down Pennsylvania Avenue. In 1995, the successor solar car, now named "GW," finished fourth in Sunrayce '95, as well as first in its class and third overall at the World Solar Rally in Japan.

explained that the activities at Goddard were concentrated on the areas of spacecraft and satellite design as well as on problems involved in communication between earth and the man-made satellites orbiting around it.

In the 1970s as well, the school started a program at Carderock, where the Navy did its main work on new ship concepts. Here, with the aid of GW professors, the Navy explored such things as how to make submarines more structurally reliable.

THE CHANGING ENVIRONMENT

During the 1970s, the computing environment in the engineering school improved tremendously. ABEL was gone,

a victim of the dramatic technological improvements in the field. In 1976, the School of Engineering and Applied Science opened its own computing facility that provided, in addition to basic number crunching, computer-aided design support, the latest in graphics capabilities, and several microcomputer laboratories. In 1983, the school received $2 million in computer equipment and software from IBM as part of the largest single-program donation in the company's history.

Three years later, in 1986, the school assumed control of the Science and Engineering Apprentice Program. This Department of Defense-sponsored program took as its goal the summer

placement in government laboratories of academically talented high school students with interest and ability in science and math. Under the direction of Marilyn Krupsaw, more than 2,500 high school students have participated in the program. Some 150 high school teachers have taken part in an affiliated program, known as Teaching New Technology, which allows them to upgrade their understanding of the working environment of scientists and engineers.

In 1993, the school took another step to solidify its relationship with the research centers in and around Washington by entering into a cooperative agreement with the National Institute of Standards and Technology. This agreement allowed GW to send graduate students to the center and to have them work on projects run by GW faculty members.

And, as these events unfolded, the school continued to be associated with cutting-edge technologies. Among the more promising breakthroughs was the student development of the solar-powered automobile, which appeared to mark a significant step toward the creation of a vehicle that would not depend on either dirty or dwindling fuel. Although the solar car remained an experimental prototype, it nonetheless attracted a great deal of media interest.

Despite these successes, engineering became a troubled field in the latter 1980s. Revenues remained flat, and expenses were increasing. In June 1994, the trustees completed a review of the situation. They affirmed the importance of engineering to GW's educational and research endeavors. After the trustees took steps to make the school, in the jargon of the day, leaner and meaner, enrollments stabilized, and efforts to secure external funds intensified.

Engineering Professor Telba Irony works through a problem with her student, Jeff Gaites, in 1994.

Engineering is a field that lends itself to change. But the changes in the engineering school have been profound. The school is probably the most international of GW's schools, with large numbers of students from Korea, Kuwait, India, Lebanon, and China, among other places. Professor Doug Jones estimates that international students make up half of the undergraduate student body.

The leadership at the school has also changed. Gideon Frieder replaced Harold Liebowitz as dean in 1993. Under Dean Frieder's leadership, the school stands poised to become a trendsetter in many areas of applied technology. In this manner, the work begun in 1884 at the Corcoran Scientific School continues into tomorrow.

Continued from p. 54

October 29, 1946, the star was disappointed to learn that the audience would be segregated. Bergman, an outspoken actress known for her liberal views, told reporters that, "Washington was a bad town in which to open a play," because of its racial discrimination.

Vincent DeAngelis, manager of Lisner, defended the University's policy as "no different from the dual system at the other Washington theaters or restaurants or schools generally." He noted that, "things will change in time."

"He didn't have anything to do with the policy," his widow, Eleanor, recently said. "Everything was separate...the public school system, the movies, the theaters. It was two separate societies."

There were pickets outside of Lisner on opening night. Less than two weeks after the show opened, two National Symphony Orchestra concerts were shifted from Lisner to nearby Constitution Hall. In 1947, after considerable debate, the trustees decided they would admit blacks to Lisner, but they would discontinue commercial theatrical performances that might draw a mixed audience. Instead, the theater would be leased to outside groups and organizations whose members, the trustees implicitly assumed, were already segregated. The decision meant that the Jim Crow system would be allowed to survive at GW; black and white audiences would not mingle on the campus.

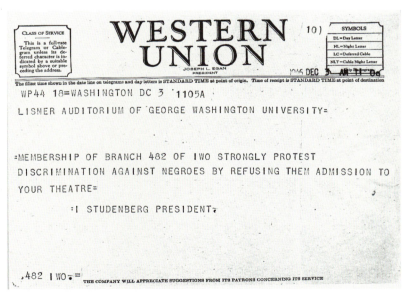

(Above) A Western Union telegram sent to Lisner Auditorium protesting segregation in the theater.

(Right) Ingrid Bergman starred in "Joan of Lorraine," which opened at Lisner Auditorium on October 29, 1949. Bergman was disappointed to learn that the audience would be segregated.

Some members of the student body protested the administration's tacit approval of segregation. On November 15, 1949, an editorial appeared in the campus paper urging the integration of the campus. The student editorial received praise in *The Washington Post* and produced a letter from Hubert Humphrey, then a first-term senator from Minnesota. "I have long felt," wrote the senator, "that the direction for progressive social change toward higher democratic values...would be provided by the youth of America. You have my congratulations and encouragement."

Humphrey's encouragement counted for little in metropolitan Washington in 1949. It took until 1954 for GW to desegregate. When it acted in July 1954, it did so at least partially because of the Supreme Court decision that spring. "Separate but equal" could no longer be the governing principle in education.

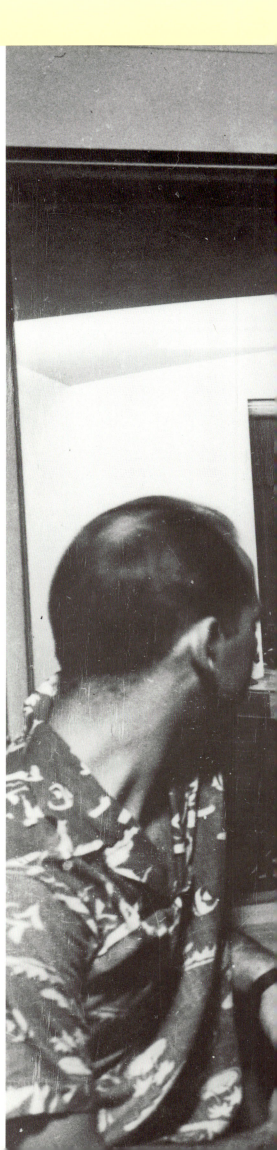

(Above) Groundbreaking for Lisner Auditorium, 1946.

(Right) The 1,490-seat Lisner Auditorium at 21st and H Streets opened its doors in 1946.

(Far right) Students in the booth at the back of Lisner Auditorium could comment on a stage production without being seen or heard by the audience, at this 1947 production.

(Left) Attending the April 7, 1955, groundbreaking ceremonies for the Tompkins Hall of Engineering were (left to right) Master Sgt. Edgar F. Auten of the University ROTC; Dean Martin A. Mason of the School of Engineering; President Marvin; Trustee Charles H. Tompkins, building donor; Trustee Robert V. Fleming; and Master Sgt. Clarence W. Voth of the University ROTC.

(Above) GW President Marvin in the University Yard with baseball letterman Bob Reid and Fritzi Nykopp, daughter of the minister to the United States from Finland.

(Right) Trustee Charles H. Tompkins takes part in breaking ground for the Tompkins Hall of Engineering, which he donated funds to build. He is shown here with President Marvin, April 7, 1955.

Whatever the motivation, classes began in 1954 with no restrictions on African-American admissions. Before this time, blacks could study only in the evening division of the University and in the post-graduate classes of the medical school. Now the entire University would be open to them. "We congratulate the University on its recent decision abolishing segregation on this campus," *The Hatchet* editorialized.

The riddle of integration was far from solved. As Washington became more and more black, the University did not respond in kind. Although blacks could attend GW, few chose to do so, and until the late 1960s, the University made only token forms of outreach to the black community. Like other parts of northwest Washington, the University remained something of a white enclave. Its isolation would be a continuing problem for administrators to address.

Still, the end of racial barriers in 1954 marked a real breakthrough, both for the University and for the city in which it resided. In the shorthand of capital commentators, Washington was becoming less a sleepy southern town and more a cosmopolitan center. GW would both influence and benefit from the increasing sophistication of Washington, D.C.

CLOYD HECK MARVIN

Decisions on integration and on nearly everything else on campus were made by Cloyd Heck Marvin, the University's president from 1927 to 1959. Under Marvin the University seemed to remain what it had always been, a small southern university, tacitly segregated, with a high-spirited student body (most of whom commuted from the suburbs).

Such appearances were deceptive. During his long tenure, Marvin increased the University's endowment from $804,000 to $7 million and tripled the size of the faculty so that it surpassed the 1,000 mark. Student enrollment nearly doubled, reaching 13,000. Among the major buildings built during Marvin's presidency were the Hall of Government, Lisner Auditorium, Strong Hall, Monroe Hall, and Tompkins Hall of Engineering. As these milestones suggest, his feats were many and prodigious.

Born on August 22, 1889, in Findlay, Ohio, Marvin attended Stanford University and then received both an undergraduate and master's degree from the University of Southern California. He completed his education at Harvard, earning an economics Ph.D. in 1919. After service as a dean at UCLA and president of the University of Arizona, he took office at GW on August 1, 1927, at age 38. Among those who recommended him was Herbert Hoover, then the Secretary of Commerce, who had close ties with Stanford and other western universities.

At GW, Marvin immediately set out to improve and expand the University's Foggy Bottom campus. In 1929, he had roses planted in the University Yard, a project in which he took a deep personal interest. Indeed, he kept his hand in nearly all aspects of the University's business. It was said that he personally supervised the landscaping and care of the grounds and personally mixed the pigments for the shade of green paint, known as Marvin green, that was used in all of the classrooms. It was Marvin who gave GW its substantial, if utilitarian, look.

Although Marvin was a great institution builder, he received increasing criticism for his political and social conservatism. During the New Deal, for example, he refused to accept financial assistance from the government, a decision that might have cost the University a chance at further expansion. He remained, like his friend Herbert Hoover, a firm opponent of federal aid.

During World War II, however, he saw the necessity of government-University cooperation and shifted the emphasis of GW activity toward government research projects. This shift led to a permanent change in University policy. In 1951, President Marvin announced

Third Washington Conference on Theoretical Physics, February 20–25, 1937. Pictured front row center is Hans Bethe. To the right are I. I. Rabi, Niels Bohr, and Felix Bloch. Behind Bohr to the right is George Gamow. In the center and toward the back, partially hidden, is Edward Teller. Both Teller and Gamow were professors at GW in the 1930s, a period which has been called the "golden years" of physics at the University. Two years later, on January 26, 1939, Niels Bohr made the first announcement of the fission of uranium at the fifth annual Washington Conference.

that, because of increased costs due to an influx of veterans, GW had begun a policy of accepting government research projects. Among the first projects was participation in the Navy Logistics Research Project and the Army's Human Resources Research Office. In 1952, Marvin dedicated Chapin Hall as the headquarters for the Air Force ROTC program.

He was less willing to shift his views on racial segregation, arguing in 1949 that it was "traditional" in Washington to follow a policy of separate but equal. In 1950, Congressman Arthur G. Klein of New York charged Marvin with an "outburst of religious and racial bigotry." The congressman had heard a news report that Marvin had threatened to fire the University's Hillel director and ban Hillel from campus. The Hillel director had supported *The Hatchet*'s pro-integration stance.

MARVIN AND THE H BOMB

Preoccupied with the details of GW's administration, Marvin did what he could to improve the quality of academic endeavors. He played a particularly important role in the development of the physics department, bringing such prominent scientists as George Gamov and Edward Teller to GW. He helped to establish the Washington Conferences on Theoretical Physics, sponsored annually by the Carnegie Institution of Washington and the University. In 1939, Niels Bohr, the Copenhagen scientist, made the first announcement of the fission of uranium at one of those meetings in the Hall of Government.

Marvin enjoyed a special relationship with Edward Teller, the brilliant Hungarian nuclear physicist. According to GW legend, the two once met in a high-ceilinged room in Foggy Bottom. "Suppose you could create a mighty force, a force that might destroy all life on earth. Do you have the right to go ahead with it?" Teller asked Marvin. "I know I can do it. I have worked out the equations."

"You can't hold back knowledge," Marvin replied, "If we don't make it, the Russians will." In this manner, Marvin attended the early phases of the birth of the hydrogen bomb.

CELEBRATING THE MARVIN ERA

In 1957, as Marvin celebrated 30 years in office, the University received special messages from J. Edgar Hoover, J. William Fulbright, and Syngman Rhee, three of its most prominent alumni.

John Edgar Hoover was born in 1895. Educated in the D.C. public schools, he graduated from GW in 1916 with a bachelor of laws and received a master of laws from the University in the following year. Deciding to remain in the District, Hoover began a career in the Department of Justice. In 1924, he became the head of the FBI, a post he held until his death in 1972. He led the nation in the quest to bring noted public enemies, such as John Dillinger, to justice. In the process, he garnered enormous publicity for himself and for the bureau.

In 1935, GW awarded J. Edgar Hoover an honorary degree. That began a 35-year period in which Hoover served on the Board of Trustees, first as an alumni trustee and then as a charter trustee. In 1970, he became an honorary trustee. When he died, the board passed a special resolution in his honor, describing him, with what some might take to be a sense of irony, as "integrity in action." Some years later, a plaque bearing Hoover's name disappeared so often from the Hoover Room at the National Law Center that the administration gave up replacing it.

Senator J. William Fulbright, LL.B. '34 the Arkansas democrat whose congressional resolution in 1943 urged U.S. adherence to a world peace organization and whose name has become synonymous with the international exchange of scholars, also honored Marvin on his completion of 30 years in office. With characteristic self-effacement, Fulbright described himself as a former student and instructor at The George Washington University. Marvin's greeting from Korean leader Syngman Rhee, GW class of '06, came at a

happier time than when GW had also awarded him an honorary degree, less than a year before his country had been invaded in 1950. The list of those who honored Marvin included a veritable who's who of cold war luminaries.

On January 28, 1959, Cloyd Heck Marvin announced his retirement from the presidency of The George Washington University. Among those who spoke in praise of Marvin was Arthur Flemming. The Secretary of Health, Education and Welfare in Eisenhower's cabinet, Flemming had received a law degree from the University in 1933. His distinguished career included service as the president of two universities as well as exemplary work in the fields of aging and civil rights.

At the end of the Marvin era, the University had formed some extraordinary connections with many other leaders of the federal establishment as well. At the same time, it remained a traditional place, one that tried to protect and shelter its students even as it encouraged those students to escape the confines of Foggy Bottom. It was also a university of grand ambitions, only some of which had been realized.

LATE FIFTIES LIFE

In the late fifties and early sixties, the University urged conservative dress on its students in part because of its location. An official explanation of the dress code in 1964 reasoned that,

> "Students at The George Washington University, located only a few blocks from the White House, represent every state in the Union and many nations. Students are observed daily by fellow students and by visitors to Washington whom they may never meet but whose impressions are formed primarily on the basis of appearance, dress, and conduct. Students are judged throughout the school year by these standards...Each student who comes to the University knows the standards of good taste. It is therefore left to the student to conduct himself within these standards. The University does not need to itemize these standards, for every gentleman knows that a shirt tail hanging out or rubber-thong sandals are not appropriate in the classroom or the public areas of the campus. For women, skirts or dresses are the only appropriate campus attire with one exception: a special provision has been made for women living in the residence halls to wear Bermuda shorts on Saturdays and Sundays. Women students must wear coats over gym clothes when travel between buildings in gym outfits becomes necessary."

The University required regular attendance at all classes and laboratories. Students could take up to three "cuts" a term, although absences immediately preceding or following a University holiday counted as two cuts. If a student missed more than a quarter of the class periods, for any reason, he or she automatically received the grade of "F."

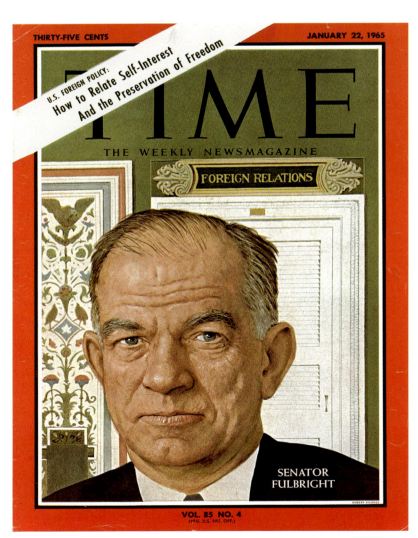

J. William Fulbright, LL.B. '34.

In 1954, Syngman Rhee, A.B. '07, president of Korea, attended a special convocation in his honor. He is shown here with President Marvin.

At the end of the Marvin era, the University still thought in grandiose terms. In March 1952, under the direction of Major General U.S. Grant III, a former vice president of the University and president of the American Planning and Civic Association, the University drafted a plan for expansion. It called for accommodating an enrollment of 50,000 and constructing many more buildings. It envisioned an almost completely enclosed University, "isolated from the urban rush and clatter, with few or no cars and traffic criss-crossing University grounds. Tasteful landscaping, including tree-shaded malls and beautiful parks and gardens will lend an air of quiet and serenity to the surroundings, so appropriate to an institution of higher learning."

Whatever else the University was in 1959, it was not serene. Traffic continued to race down its streets. Enrollment, far from reaching 50,000, remained closer to 10,000, making GW the second largest university in the D.C. area, after the University of Maryland. Admission was on a modestly selective basis. In 1959, word came that for the first time, admissions officers would require applicants to take the Scholastic Aptitude Test. Marvin had developed a durable structure; it remained for others to push the University toward excellence.

The Weather

Today and tonight — Cloudy. Chance of scattered showers. High in mid-90s; low in low 70s. Tuesday — Cloudy, hot and humid. Sunday's high, 90 at 3:00 p.m.; low, 68 at 7:10 a.m.

Weather Map and Details on Page B4.

The Washington

Times Herald

LIBRARY

87th Year .. No. 242   Phone RE. 7-1234

Copyright © 1964
The Washington Post Co.

MONDAY, AUGUST 3, 1964

U.S. Destroyer Fights Off
In Attack Off Coast of Nort

Moon Probe Evaluation Now Begins

Scientific Study Of 4000 Photos May Take Years

By Ralph Dighton

PASADENA, Calif., Aug. 2 (AP)—This week — and probably for years to come —space scientists will pore over the historic moon photographs that Ranger 7 relayed to earth Friday with costly miniatures of the cameras that produce pictures on home television ...

... he photographs released ...y night were the best ...d in a quick review of ...than 4000 snapped in the ...13 minutes and 40 sec...s Ranger 7 plunged to ...ction.

...nning Monday the oth... will be studied to de... (1) whether any part ...200,000 square miles ...phed would be a good ...ite for manned Apol... ...ips, and (2) whether ...efinement is neces... ...e spacecraft's tele... ...em.

...eam Cone

...m, overhauled ex... ...er Ranger C failed ...ures before it hit ...ast February, is ...vel of engineer...

CAPT. J. J. HERRICK

Above is a photograph of the Navy destroyer Maddox, which was attacked yesterday with torpedoes and gunfire from three North Vietnamese PT boats in the Gulf of Tonkin off Viet-Nam. At left is Navy Capt. John J. Herrick, of Minne-

apolis, Minn., commander of Destroyer Division 192, who was aboard the Maddox, the Division's flagship, at the time of the attack. Cmdr. Herbert L. Ogier Jr., at right, is commanding officer of the Maddox. He is from St. Petersburg, Fla.

CMDR. H. L. OGIER J

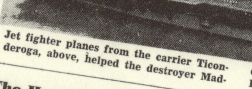

Jet fighter planes from the carrier Ticonderoga, above, helped the destroyer Mad-

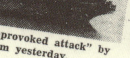

dox beat off the "unprovoked attack" by PT boats off Viet-Nam yesterday.

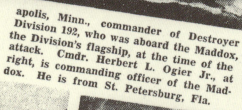

Navy Crusader jet fighter similar to those used yesterday in fighting off the PT boat attacks.

The Harris Survey

Humphrey Is Favorite of Democrats
Since President Eliminated Kennedy

By Louis Harris

© 1964, The Washington Post Co.

When President Johnson eliminated Attorney General Robert Kennedy and other key members of his Administration from consideration as vice presidential candidates, he catapulted Sen. Hubert Humphrey into a commar... lead ...

tial race, here is how possible candidates now line up among rank-and-file Democrats:

DEMOCRATS' CURRENT CHOICE FOR VICE PRESIDENT

Total ...

Humphrey was rising as the President made his decision. Attorney General Kennedy still held a substantial lead, but his backing appeared to be ebbing.

The negot...

COMMUNIST CHINA

NORTH VIET-NAM

Kwantung Province

LAOS

Hanoi

Plain of Jars

Gulf of Tonkin

Vientiane

Vinh

Haikou

The Changing Campus

INTERLUDE:

THE PRESIDENCY OF THOMAS CARROLL

During a brief interregnum, Dean Oswald Colclough served as acting president, and then, in the summer of 1960, the trustees selected Thomas Henry Carroll as GW's new president. One trustee commented, "We have a good University, but it isn't what it ought to be." Thomas Carroll came to set things right.

Time magazine described him as "the holder of one of the most impressive resumes ever scrutinized by a board of college trustees," and, indeed, his credentials were impressive. Born in San Francisco, a descendant of the Carroll family of great social prominence in Maryland, he graduated from the University of California (Berkeley) in 1934 and received a master's degree in 1936 and a Ph.D. in 1939 from Harvard Business School. He began his career teaching at Harvard. After military service in World War II, he became dean of the College of Business Administration at Syracuse. In 1950, at the age of 36, he became dean and professor in the School of Business Administration at the University of North Carolina. In 1954, he was appointed a vice president of the Ford Foundation, at a time when that giant philanthropic organization was just getting organized.

A tall and broad-shouldered man, he described himself, in a wonderfully self-deprecating manner, as "outstandingly non-athletic." Despite this modesty, *The New York Times* noted that many in Washington "considered (him) a new type of university president... a young and attractive intellectual with the aplomb of a diplomat, a broad academic and administrative background and thorough fund-raising and financial experience."

(Below) Then-Congressman Daniel Inouye, J.D. '52, of Hawaii (second from the left) at an alumni dinner in 1961 with (left to right) *Sen. Jack R. Miller of Iowa, Congressman Joe L. Evins of Tennessee, and GW President Thomas Carroll.*

(Above) President Carroll's inauguration ceremony took place on a bright day in the University Yard *on May 3, 1961. Carroll became the 13th president of the University.*

MR. KENNEDY COMES TO CALL

Carroll's inauguration as president was among the most spectacular events in the history of the University. President John F. Kennedy disliked wearing hats, but he made an exception on May 3, 1961. On that day, he and his wife drove the few blocks from the White House to the University Yard in back of Lisner.

When the president of the United States and the first lady arrived, they found themselves among 2,000 students, educators, and guests who watched as the president, in a black academic gown, a purple hood, and a mortar board, received an honorary degree. Kennedy gave a short speech on the cold war, always one of his favorite subjects and, in the season of the Bay of Pigs, one that was very much on his mind. He noted that it was the job of schools and colleges "to provide the men and women who will, with their sense of discipline and purpose and understanding, contribute to the maintenance of free societies here and around the world..."

John F. Kennedy addressed the GW crowd with his customary charm. He told the story of how once, at Harvard University, somebody came around and asked for President Lowell. "He's in

(Left) John F. Kennedy (left) spoke at President Carroll's inauguration. Carroll's presidency brought a spark to the University that lasted until his untimely death in 1964. Ironically, Kennedy's death pre- *ceded Carroll's. Kennedy attended the ceremony with his wife, First Lady Jackie Kennedy (shown above), who earned her A.B. from GW in 1951.*

Washington seeing Mr. Taft," was the reply. The president suggested that someone would soon ask to see the new president of George Washington, only to be told that he was over at the White House seeing Mr. Kennedy.

Then President Kennedy told a more personal anecdote. Accepting his honorary degree, his first as president, he announced that his "wife had beaten him to the honor by several years, but it took her two years to get a degree, and it took me two minutes; but in any case, we are both grateful." The president was referring to the fact that Jacqueline Bouvier, after studying at Vassar and at the Sorbonne, attended GW in the early 1950s and received an A.B. in 1951. The connection between the University and its White House neighbors remained close.

THE CARROLL ERA

In many ways, GW in the Carroll era resembled the University in the Marvin era. Curricular reform proceeded apace. On May 16, 1961, for example, the Board of Trustees abolished the Junior College for freshmen and sophomores. Instead of having to obtain an Associate of Arts degree before they could matriculate as juniors, students would now receive a certificate indicating that they had completed the necessary prerequisites.

Other aspects of student life also changed. Beginning in 1961, students received identification cards in their registration packets. Before this time, the only means of student identification was a crumpled pink registration slip or a bulky student activities book. The ID card replaced both the pink slip and the activities book. In September 1963, another amenity arrived: the University agreed to cash students' personal checks, although the limit was $25.

These were at best superficial changes. The campus in 1962 offered few hints of the turmoil that would ensue at the end of the decade. In a typical piece of student journalism, *The Hatchet* ran an editorial in January 1962 praising the Young Democrats and the Young Republicans for their role in combating political apathy among the student body. The paper praised the Young Republicans for their decision to invite Senator Barry Goldwater to speak. "It is commendable," wrote the editorial board, "that the YRs are willing to take the necessary initiative to give the University a big-time intellectual atmosphere that it should have to be able to live up to its position in the nation's capital." The paper urged students to lend their attendance and enthusiasm to the effort.

What signs of activity there were bore a close resemblance to the panty raids, phone-booth-stuffing stunts, and goldfish-eating contests that characterized the 1950s. At three in the morning on October 30, 1962, some eager Alpha Epsilon Pi pledges painted an intersection on campus with the words, "AEPi says Back Army in Cuba—Beat them on the Grid." This sentiment concerning the Cuban missile crisis and the fortunes of the GW football team led to a minor riot when police requested that the pledges scrub their slogan off the street. Three of the participants were arrested. The incident, which took place on the corner of 21st and G Streets, became known as the G Street riot.

President Carroll turned his mind toward more serious matters. At the December 1962 meeting of the Board of Trustees, he discussed the need to make GW a leader in helping the city cope with changes in its public schools. He noted that these schools contained, for the first time, a majority of black students and worried that GW's education school had not done enough to plan for the future of those schools.

THE SUPERDORM ARRIVES

Although President Carroll might have preferred to concentrate on intellectual and public policy issues, much of his time was taken up with plans for the expansion of the University's physical plant. In the spring of 1963, the University purchased the Park Central Apartments. On July 23, 1963, came word that the University would convert these apartments, located at 19th and F Streets, into the Washington area's largest college dormitory, scheduled to open in September 1964. Authorities figured that the nine-story building, constructed in 1930, could house 1,000 students. The decision was made to turn Thurston Hall, as the facility would soon be called, into a women's dormitory. Once the 317 apartments were made into dorm rooms, there would be space available for all female undergraduates to live on campus. The kitchens would become study rooms. The University would add a dining room to the facility capable of seating 400 students (only one of the University's six dorms had dining facilities at the time).

As always, the trustees turned their attention to creating a master plan to guide the University's expansion. In June 1964, they decided to hire an architectural firm to prepare such a plan. It was one of the tragedies of GW history that Thomas Carroll, who received such a glittering send-off, never lived to fulfill his promise. In the summer of 1964, at the age of 50, he learned that he had heart trouble. The doctors advised rest. On July 27, 1964, on vacation in a secluded mountain cabin, he died of a heart attack.

During Thomas Carroll's brief tenure, the University enrollment increased about 21 percent, to 11,000. The University raised the number of its student residence facilities and established an Institute for Sino-Soviet Studies that would undertake the sort of cold war studies of which President Kennedy so approved. But neither Kennedy nor Carroll lived long enough to see the results of these studies. And Carroll did not have the pleasure of attending the opening of Thurston Hall in September 1964.

The "Superdorm," Thurston Hall,
located on the southwest corner of
19th and F Streets.

LYNDA BIRD

In 1964, Washington's rhythm changed to accommodate the presidential election, one that had been drastically altered by Kennedy's assassination. Lyndon Johnson, sworn in as president by Judge Sarah Tilghman Hughes, LL.B. '22, decided that he would like to have his family live with him in the White House. That decision prompted Lynda Bird Johnson to transfer to GW from the University of Texas, beginning in spring semester 1964.

Once again, a daughter of a president graced the GW campus. During the 1964 election campaign, the junior history major accompanied her mother on the Lady Bird Special, whistle-stopping across the south, and flew west for a special visit to the Oklahoma State Homecoming. Throughout all of this activity, Lynda Bird Johnson conscientiously kept up with her studies. She was reported to be reading Garrett Mattingly's *The Armada*, assigned in Professor Robert Kenny's English history course, on the campaign trail. Another GW history professor recalled an invitation from Lynda to visit the White House and of being introduced to Lyndon Johnson. The president greeted the GW prof effusively and thanked him for the education Lynda Bird was getting. In 1992, she was elected an honorary member of Phi Beta Kappa.

THE ELLIOTT YEARS BEGIN

Throughout the campaign and the spring semester of 1965, the University searched for a new president. As the search continued, Dean Colclough once again agreed to serve as president on an interim basis, and once again he did an able job. By the end of the semester, the trustees had settled on Lloyd Hartman Elliott, the president of the University of Maine, as GW's next president.

After the patrician Carroll, Elliott's background appeared to be decidedly humble. He was born on a farm in Clay County, West Virginia, in 1918. In addition to running the 150-acre farm, his father also served as the local schoolmaster. Elliott himself began his education in a one-room ungraded school house. Working at his own pace, he managed to graduate from the eighth grade at the age of 10. He finished at Glenville State College in 1937, still well ahead of the others in his age cohort. In college, he served as sports editor of the newspaper and participated enthusiastically in intercollegiate athletics, earning letters in basketball, tennis, and baseball. He remained a passionate advocate of physical fitness and, during his long tenure at GW, which lasted until 1988, Elliott could often be found in the gym playing handball or a competitive game of pickup basketball.

(Left) Lynda Bird Johnson (center) attended the University while her father was in office. Provost (and soon-to-be-acting president) Oswald S. Colclough greets Lynda and her friend, Warrie Lynn Smith, on their way to class on Feb. 3, 1964.

(Right) GW's Washington, D.C., location has made the University the perfect place for students to learn about politics first hand. Jack Miller of the Young Democrats is shown here handing out literature in the 1964 Mock Election at GW.

Lloyd Elliott chose a career in education. He received his master's degree in 1939 from West Virginia University and then became first a teacher and later a principal in the Widen, West Virginia, public schools. If World War II had not intervened, he might have stayed there. But instead he went into the Navy and rose to the rank of lieutenant commander. He saw substantial combat action during the war, including harrowing duty in command of a tank craft that was wrecked in a storm during the invasion of Sicily. Liberated from the service in 1946, he decided to go to Colorado. There he pursued doctoral studies in education at the University of Colorado and became an assistant superintendent of the Boulder, Colorado, public schools.

In 1948, Elliott received his Ed.D. and accepted a job at Cornell as an assistant professor of educational administration. Once again, his rise was rapid. Within four years he had become a full professor, a sign of the fluid situation in American universities in the postwar era and of Elliott's impressive abilities. Soon after achieving the top professorial rank, Elliott became enmeshed in administrative duties. Between 1956 and 1958, he served as the executive assistant to Cornell's president before he was tapped in 1958 to become the president of the University of Maine.

Elliott's appointment at GW did not meet with universal approval. The University Faculty Assembly resented the manner in which he was selected and knew little about him, except that his academic background was in education. On June 8, 1965, the assembly passed a resolution opposing his selection.

When Elliott arrived in August, he was very much aware of the faculty's concerns about him. In typical fashion, he met with the faculty leaders and soon gained their resounding approval. During the rest of his tenure, which occurred at what might have been the most contentious period in the history of American higher education, relations between the faculty and the president remained cordial.

In part that was attributable to Elliott's management style. Although he could be tough and often described himself as stubborn, he did not commit the sin of micromanagement. Unlike Cloyd Marvin, who tried to gain control over each and every University operation, Lloyd Elliott believed in giving his deans and administrators considerable freedom to operate within their own bailiwicks. At the same time, the president worked hard to raise the University's prestige and to develop the necessary infrastructure for a productive research university.

(Left) President Lloyd Elliott crowns Sheila Miller as 1965 Homecoming Queen.

(Top right) President Elliott enjoyed an occasional game of hoops in the Smith Center.

The University that Elliott inherited contained, for the first time in its modern history, a preponderance of graduate and professional students. The president realized that these students, and their undergraduate counterparts, required a first-rate library. He was dismayed by what he found at GW. The library continued to be housed in Lisner Hall, with a rickety elevator and cramped book stacks. Hours were limited. Well into the 1950s, for example, the library opened only four hours a day on weekends. It closed at one o'clock on Saturdays and did not reopen until two o'clock on Sundays.

On one of Elliott's first visits to GW before being inaugurated as president, he arranged to take a tour of the library with John Russell Mason, the chief librarian. The two went through the stacks, climbing over piles of books and manuscripts. Sometime during the tour, Mason turned to Elliott and in a somewhat exasperated voice said, "Dr. Elliott, we can't buy any more books because we don't have any place to put them." Elliott, characteristically, said nothing, but thought to himself that the library was inappropriate for a university of GW's scope and stature. He seized on the improvement of the library as one of his administration's goals.

IN LOCO PARENTIS

Despite the increasing importance of graduate and professional study at GW, Elliott spent much of his first five years at GW contending with the issues of undergraduate student life. It was a time of transition from the era of *in loco parentis*, in which a university acted as the parent's surrogate in the protection of the students under its care, to the era of *laissez faire*, in which a university granted students increased freedom and treated them, in effect, as adults.

When Elliott arrived on campus, students had some basic grievances with the administration over the freedoms they should be allowed. First-year undergraduate women still were not allowed out after 11 p.m. during the week. In the social or "date rooms" of the dorms, women were not allowed to wear slacks. Nor were upperclass women permitted to live off campus. Instead, they were required to live at home with their parents or in a University dorm, such as Strong Hall. That rule rankled them because upperclass men were allowed to live off campus. Beginning in 1965, however, the University's policy changed to permit junior and senior women to live off campus. First, however, they had to petition the dean of women "for permission to live with their own contemporaries." Within a few years, the rule had become relaxed to the extent that, in fall 1969, unmarried sophomore women were allowed to live off campus.

(Above) Students spent many hours studying in the Main Reading Room of the old University Library (1920). (Right) Students in the Lisner Hall library in 1963. This library served GW until 1973, when the Gelman Library opened its doors.

Rules about "overnights" also occasioned conflict and controversy. In the fall of 1965, GW still required all female residents to submit parental permission slips at the beginning of each year. That gave parents the opportunity to instruct University authorities as to whether their daughters could enjoy "sign-out privileges." Parents had the option of granting blanket permission, allowing their daughter, in the words of one University publication, "to select hostesses at her own discretion," or to specify the places where their daughter might spend the night. Freshman women could have only five overnights per semester, and even those required that they submit permission slips 24 hours in advance of their departure. It was strict University policy that first-year undergraduate women be in their dorms by one in the morning on Saturdays and Sundays.

Sex and sexual equality were subjects on which GW had no official opinion. In 1966, a 19-year-old sophomore "coed," as female students were described at the time, walked into the student health service on a Thursday and calmly requested a prescription for Enovid, a popular birth control pill. The physician on duty told the student that, "We wouldn't give you any...we're unofficially opposed to it." Whether the physician meant oral contraception or sexual intercourse was unclear. That same year an enterprising *Hatchet* editor asked Paul Bissell, the dean of men, and Virginia Kirkbride, the dean of women, why men were allowed to drink in dorms and women were not. Encapsulating the conventional wisdom of the time, Dean Bissell replied, "men and women are different."

Beyond the immediate issues of the campus, the first year of Elliott's presidency coincided with a major escalation of the Vietnam War. At GW, the war elicited little comment. Those who did speak out tended to support Lyndon Johnson. In the fall of 1965, the residents of Welling Hall, many of whom were athletes, launched an all-out campaign to demonstrate their support for LBJ's Vietnam policy. As Bob Detore, Welling Hall president, put it, "The war in Vietnam is an ugly war, a cruel war, but it is a war we must win. We ask that everyone on campus join with us, not for our sake, but for the sake of the country."

The very next semester the administration granted a two-month trial charter for a GW chapter of the Students for a Democratic Society (SDS). Chapter head Charles Cover, far from presenting himself as a typical radical, portrayed the SDS program at GW in very modest terms. The first program organized by SDS featured a discussion of the place of the writer in American society. Cover said that the program would include a diversity of viewpoints so as to present the issue in an interesting way. After that, Cover hoped, students might go home and discuss such things as artistic alienation with their roommates. As late as spring 1966, therefore, the student revolution showed few signs of arriving on the campus of GW.

Two entering freshmen review the University publication Academic Guide for Entering Freshmen.

The Law School

Sparking reader interest in the GW law school's first hundred years would put a strain on any narrator. The early history is touched upon here, but even a fast-forward narration can't match for reader appeal the exciting events of the past 30 years.

Vignettes offer fascinating, if sometimes lurid, glimpses of what it meant to be associated—in recent times—with the National Law Center. Here, for example, at the height of the Vietnam War is law professor Monroe Friedman burning his draft card on the back steps of Lisner to the cheers of anti-war demonstrators. Here is law professor John Banzhaf remarking calmly: "It doesn't surprise me" on hearing that three of his students have won a public interest suit forcing Spiro Agnew, a sitting vice president, to pay back $270,000 to the citizens of Maryland for kickbacks he

received. Or the spectacle of Chief Justice Warren Burger weighing into the battle to "save the GW night school" in 1984.

During Watergate, on the lurid side, no fewer than seven GW law alumni figured in the hearings. Some were heroes, like tough-minded special prosecutor Leon Jaworski; or Alexander Butterfield, who disclosed the existence of the Nixon tapes; or Acting FBI Director L. Patrick Gray, who turned over FBI files on Watergate to a bean-spilling John Dean. (From that point on, the end was in sight.) Maybe others were not so heroic,

(Above) Columbian University building and law school (the building on the left), located at 15th and H Streets, circa 1910.

(Left) The law school resided in this building—originally Trinity Church—located on 5th Street, from 1865-1884.

like special counsel Charles Colson Jr., stonewaller and master of denial, and James McCord, Jr., the security coordinator for CREEP (Committee to Re-elect the President) who was arrested with four others for the Watergate break-in.

But if guilt by association is hard to swallow, self-esteem by association is more palatable. Thus, developments on GW's law school front have always been attended by a certain degree of boosterism, some of it self generated, but much of it well deserved. On one hand, for example, alumni at the school's 50th anniversary could read in a commemorative pamphlet how "a vast army of alumni spreading over the face of the nation and extending to the islands of the seas has gone forth to carry the word that their Alma Mater is teaching the science of law in a scholarly manner."

The law school from 1921-1925
was housed at 1435 K Street.

The writer got the last four words right, certainly: "in a scholarly manner." The GW law faculty, even in their early years, produced some noteworthy scholarly "firsts." In 1877, they offered the nation's first graduate-level program for a Master of Laws degree. In the late 19th century, they reportedly invented the first moot court, or trial practice as they called it, offering students the sort of simulated courtroom experience that is still widely imitated. And if not first, certainly right up there (by 1915), the school had designated a portion of its faculty to do research in addition to teaching.

THE FALSE START, 1826-27

Legal education at GW (it was Columbian College then) got off to a rocky start in 1826. Its two professors could hardly be called a "faculty" when William Cranch, chief justice of the U.S. Circuit Court, gave his inaugural lecture in the courtroom at city hall on June 12. Cranch and a law clerk named William Carroll were the school's only professors of law, and their paychecks ran out a year later.

Only from 1865 can today's National Law Center date an unbroken continuum. But the date of origin, 1865, nonetheless marks the law school as the oldest in the District of Columbia.

THE GENDER ISSUE

In its beginnings, and until the turn of the century, the school quietly went about preparing anyone who'd had a year or two of college for the bar exam. Anyone, that is, except women and blacks. The law faculty in 1883 found that legal training for women was "not required by any public want," a view

perhaps inspired by the 1880 census count of only 75 women lawyers in the entire country.

Earlier, in 1869, the law school reportedly rejected the application of longtime Washington feminist Belva Ann Lockwood, who later received her law degree at the now-defunct National University, which GW took over in 1954. A reporter for the *Washington News*, describing Lockwood as "irrepressible," noted with a touch of 19th-century sexism that "the idea of female students met with approbation from many of the sterner sex, who are doubtless contemplating what pleasures they will have in going through the mazes of legal disquisitions in the company of the fair and lovely characters whose presence in the schoolroom will be so comforting."

Not until the eve of World War I were women admitted to the law school. On February 10, 1914, the law faculty solemnly resolved that women be permitted to register "on the same terms that men are admitted, provided their admission be approved by the president of the University." Marion Clark was the first woman to graduate with a GW LL.B., in 1916.

Subsequent developments corrected these deficiencies in dramatic ways. Sixty-seven years later, alumna Teresa Moran Schwartz, NLC class of '71, became the center's first associate dean of students.

In 1960, Patricia Roberts Harris, the daughter of a dining car waiter, received her J.D. and won the John Bell Larner Award for graduating first in her class. Her rise after GW was steep. She worked in the Criminal Division of the Department of Justice and then became

dean of students at the Howard University Law School. Between 1965 and 1967, she served as United States Ambassador to Luxembourg. Returning to Howard, she taught law and then in 1969 became dean. After a stint in private practice, she served in President Jimmy Carter's cabinet, first as Secretary of Housing and Urban Development and later as Secretary of Health and Human Services. After an unsuccessful attempt to become Washington's mayor, she returned to GW and served with great distinction as a professor in the National Law Center. It was a career filled with accomplishment, but one cut short by her death on March 23, 1985.

FACULTY AND STUDENTS

Of timeless concern to all educational institutions is the visibility of their faculty, their ability to draw the big names, who in turn will attract students by promising intellectual contact with the most distinguished members of their calling. Capitalizing on its location, the law school found no shortage of legal luminaries to grace its lecture halls in the late 19th century. Some still have name recognition—three Supreme Court justices (Harlan, Brewer, and Strong); the former diplomat Caleb Cushing, who negotiated our first treaty with China; legal historian Francis Wharton; and such prominent political figures as George Ticknor Curtis and Henry St. George Tucker.

Faculty of the National Law Center today may be less interested in big-name recognition than in renown gained for innovating, specializing, and carving out a national reputation for legal activism, a pursuit enhanced by an equally activist student body. Though faculty have

(From the top) Belva Lockwood was one of the first two women to graduate from the law school.

Teresa Moran Schwartz, J.D. '71, became the law school's first associate dean of students in 1981.

sometimes engaged their students in spirited disagreement, they have always listened.

A good example of constructive listening came in the turbulent '60s when student discourse elsewhere on campus ranged from uncivil to riotous. At a time when faculty and administrators often exchanged indignities with student activists chanting "student power" and making "non-negotiable demands," relative calm appears to have prevailed at the law school. Though GW law students were as reformist as any, law professor James Starrs credits their willingness to work within, rather than disrupt, "the system" with making some much-needed changes. Led by third-year law student Larry Adlerstein (whom Starrs called a "true free spirit"), students and faculty nudged one another to make revisions in the curriculum, evaluate courses, hold student forums, and become active in good causes. Adlerstein's campaign to persuade faculty to switch from the LL.B. to the Juris Doctorate degree bore fruit in November 1967 when the faculty in closed session so resolved.

LEGAL ACTIVISM IN THE '60S AND '70S

John Banzhaf's "Bandits," whose acronymic forays into legal activism included SOUP, PUMP, CRASH, TUBE, and ASH (Students Opposing Unfair Practices, Protesting Unfair Marketing Practices, Citizens to Restrict Airline Smoking Hazards, Terminating Unfair Broadcasting Exercises, and Action on Smoking and Health, respectively), knowingly or not, built on a GW tradition of community betterment that dates from 1914, when the law school established its first legal aid society. When Nancy Puffenbarger published an account of GW's newest phase of legal activism (*GWU Magazine*, Spring 1970), she provided a veritable reader's guide to the school's incredibly diverse array of student-professor outreach bent on righting the wrongs of the societal status quo.

While many radicalized students of the late '60s sought to lobotomize their universities from within, the school's activists looked outward with a view to accomplishing what might be called surgical reconstruction. Students in Professor Banzhaf's class on unfair trade practices, to quote Puffenbarger, "attacked consumer abuses ranging from false weighing of canned string beans to unfair broadcasting practices." Banzhaf was not alone. Professors Arthur Miller, Donald Rothschild, Monroe Friedman, Robert Dixon, James Starrs, and Jerome Barron all engaged their students in one or more external enterprises. The work of Eric Sirulnik, who directed a wide array of community legal clinics, was critical in this regard.

By 1970, Starrs was quoted as saying, "I've never seen, in any university I've been in, such a willingness to allow diversity in its faculty and programs. It's way ahead of Harvard in its poverty programs. GW was first with its housing programs, its Students-in-Court Program, and the like." When Starrs was interviewed, more than 200 GW law student volunteers were getting an astonishing variety of practical experience in the school's Legal Aid Bureau. They had choices—they could participate in a juvenile court program, answer legal questions from prisoners, give lectures at nearby high schools, counsel indigents,

assist poverty lawyers, track abusive police practices, or deal with violations of civil rights.

Above all, activism in the late '60s energized the curriculum, multiplying courses, programs, and clinics almost faster than they could be named. Ralph Nader guest lectured at GW, and Dean Robert Kramer noted that private lawyers wrote to him almost daily offering to give courses. Commenting on the phenomenon, Kramer said, "I don't think there's a better location in the world for a law school. We can offer an incredible number of courses. We have a strong, young faculty who can be satisfied here."

(Left) GW law students have been providing legal counsel to the community since 1914, with the inception of its first legal aid society. Today, the National Law Center's community legal clinics continue this tradition.

(Above) The law school attracts a diverse student body. Shown here in 1992 (left to right): Black Law Students Association (BLSA) Vice President Karlton Butts; active duty naval officer John Jenkins Jr.; Student Bar Association (SBA) Vice President Tracy DuPree; Asian Pacific American Law Student Association President Amy Huang; BLSA President Rebecca Taylor; and SBA President Kathleen Cahill.

(Above) Law Professor Thomas Buergenthal leads the National Law Center's Government program in international and comparative law. A Holocaust survivor, Prof. Buergenthal has been a prominent writer and advocate for the protection of international human rights. As an activist, he served as a judge and president of the Inter-American Court of Human Rights.

(Right) Professor James Starrs is usually on the scene when controversial forensic evidence comes under public scrutiny.

Ten years later, in 1980, with the fires of activism still burning, the school opened one of three clinics in the country dealing with immigration. Afghanis seeking asylum, aliens facing deportation, and (for third-year students) the possibility of representing clients at hearings before the Immigration and Naturalization Service, all spoke to the now well-established impulse to meet contemporary problems with timely legal education and practice. Three years later, GW's new Consumer Litigation Center was training students to try cases of product misrepresentation, or, when the law proved helpless, catch the public's attention by airing "consumer cases" in the media. That same year, two law professors, two students, and an alumnus, working with the National Organization for the Reform of Marijuana Laws (NORML), won a court injunction to stop the Drug Enforcement Administration from spraying paraquat on national forest lands.

In the near neighborhood, meanwhile, one of the school's clinics made headlines in *The Washington Star* (January 3, 1979) for achieving a near monopoly in advising the city's poor on what to do about their financial problems. The lead paragraph put it succinctly: "One lawyer and nine law students, charging $6 per case, have cornered a major share of the market of personal bankruptcy cases in the District of Columbia." Clinic head Richard Willis explained that while his students handled no business bankruptcies, they had thus far helped 52 individuals "who have gone way over their heads and need to get out of a cycle of bad debts."

THE NIGHT SCHOOL CONTROVERSY

Divisive issues, while they sometimes put students and faculty at odds, occasionally brought alumni and trustees into the fray. Such was the "night school" controversy.

This debate wasn't really about closing down evening classes, although it veered in that direction. It was about whether part-time students should meet the same academic standards as full-time students. Because the standards were allegedly lower for part-time admittees—and most of them attended evening classes—the controversy was misperceived as an attack on the "night school," rather than as an effort to upgrade standards.

Long smoldering, the debate over the future of GW's "evening division" first surfaced in 1978 when a self study headed by Professor Glen Weston refuted a nationwide study that characterized law schools with evening divisions as inherently second-rank, less prestigious than those without. Weston countered that while "evening programs" elsewhere might be substandard, GW's attracted students who were mature, ambitious, and highly motivated. And in keeping with the times, he noted they also offered opportunities for minority students to enter the profession. Nor were evening students, as some charged, more prone to lapses in professional ethics. Weston wrote: "We have had our Charles Colson (evening), but Georgetown has had its John Dean (day)...of instances that have come to my attention of disbarment, suspension, or conviction of our graduates in Maryland, D.C., and Virginia, four have involved day graduates and two have involved evening students." Moreover, if the school dropped its night students,

Weston warned, it would have to recruit 300 more day students and raise tuition by about $1,000 a year. The controversy subsided, but only briefly.

In January 1980, *The Hatchet* reported that although faculty denied it, evening courses were seen to be inferior. Professor Harold Green, whose faculty committee was urging an end to them, pointed to the difficulty of recruiting top-flight faculty and of placing night students with major law firms. The perception of inferiority was "deplorable," he said, "but a very real one." Only six of the top 60 law schools still had evening programs.

Weston's defense apparently failed to convince the faculty. Six years later, they voted overwhelmingly to phase out admissions to the evening division J.D. program. Their decision evoked a storm of protest. An apparent attack on the "night school" brought more than a thousand letters from outraged alumni,

spirited testimonials, and angry charges of elitism. The trustees split openly on the issue, and Dean Jerome Barron, caught in the middle, allowed cautiously to *The Hatchet* that he was "open-minded on it." Only gradually did the key issue become clear. It was not whether night classes would continue—they would—but whether uniform standards should be applied to all applicants—they should. Once the parties realized that the question was one of standards and not whether classes should meet before or after sunset, they easily "compromised" in favor of uniform standards.

THE RACE ISSUE

Nobody said much about the unblinking whiteness of GW's student (and faculty) population when it began to be noticeable in the '40s and '50s. Some, like law applicant Daniel Inouye, discovered how fully segregated GW was only after he was admitted. Reminiscing quietly in his Senate office, Inouye told how he had applied to GW's law school in 1950 more

for its location than its reputation. Hawaii was not yet a state, and, though inclined toward a political career, he had no plans for entering Congress. When he found out the campus was segregated, he said his first impulse was to leave. When he asked the dean for an explanation, he was told that donors whose gifts built the dormitories had stipulated they be segregated. In a later, more enlightened era, Inouye became a trustee of the University.

In 1968, GW and New York University received the first Office of Economic Opportunity grants to set up poverty law programs. That same year, as the wave of student activism crested—the National Law Center undertook a vigorous campaign to recruit minorities.

In addition to library materials, the Jacob Burns Law Library building houses faculty and student-organization offices. The reading room is shown here.

The final touches were completed on the Jacob Burns Law Library in 1984, thanks to the generosity of alumnus Jacob Burns, LL.B. '24, LL.D. '70.

ties. "I don't feel defensive about our [recruiting] program," he said. "It's been a damned honest effort to provide an opportunity to those who would not have had a chance." A year later the complaint was quietly dropped.

In early 1979, a stalled dean search outside the University led Elliott to appoint Professor Jerome Barron as dean, an insider whose appointment, though confirmed by the search committee and subsequently by the faculty, raised charges that the president had acted "autocratically." Those who complained made clear their quarrel was not with Barron, for whom, *The Hatchet* reported, they had "the greatest personal respect," but with the administration. Faculty fussing aside, it was Barron who led the school through its stormy "night school" controversy and presided over its major expansion of physical plant.

THE NATIONAL LAW CENTER

Christened in 1959, the National Law Center was an idea looking for a home. President Marvin's original plans had a certain grandeur. On May 10, 1949, when he told the law alumni his plans for a National Law Center, the president said he envisioned a building eight-stories tall covering an entire city block. Academically, his plans envisioned an aggregation of "judges, lawyers of all specialties, teachers, and both graduate and undergraduate law students, who would come together to work on problems not only affecting the entire profession, but also the welfare of the nation."

Three years later, its 61 black students placed it second only to Harvard in numbers. Successful recruitment, however, came not without attendant controversy.

In 1974, black students filed a complaint with the D.C. Human Rights Commission, charging they had been victimized by discriminatory grading practices; failing grades among blacks had been disproportionately high. Specifically, the complaint alluded to "professors who are known by all black students...to be biased in their appraisal of blacks' academic work." Dean Edward Potts flatly denied the charge, stating, "I do not know of any member of this faculty who would discriminate against blacks in grading," and cited the "anonymous" grading system as proof against its occurring. The complaint went on to recount student efforts to get statistics on grading disparities—statistics which Potts said were not available. If disparities did exist, Potts suggested they lay in the somewhat lower admission standards for disadvantaged minori-

Adjunct Professor Benjamin H. Grumbles, an attorney with the House Subcommittee on Water Resources, shares an insider's perspective with his class on water pollution control.

Early planners admitted from the outset that the "financial aspects" had not yet been worked out. It took Marvin four years to initiate a fund-raising campaign, but once it started he promised construction would begin in 1955.

Time passed and funding efforts lagged. In May 1960, Dean Charles Nutting predicted completion by 1965, the law school's centennial year. Explaining past delays, Nutting noted how steeply construction costs had risen. Marvin's 1949 estimate of $4.5 million, he noted, was now closer to $10 million. Twenty years later, when Lloyd Elliott decided to set aside Marvin's plans altogether, the guesstimate had climbed to $25 million. Had it been built, the center building would have been located "in the area bordered by Pennsylvania Avenue."

When Elliott decided instead to build brackets on Stockton Hall, faculty were quick to claim they had been left out of the planning process. Albeit briefly, they joined in one of those time-honored disputes as to where the line should be drawn between faculty consultation and final decision making. Only briefly, however. Faced with Elliott's *fait accompli*, they and the Student Bar Association promptly came forward with a "needs list" (more offices, library reading space, carpeting, etc.).

Building plans finally came to fruition in the spring of 1984. Where Bacon Hall had once leaned comfortably against the north side of Stockton, the Theodore Lerner building opened for classes at the corner of H and 20th. It provided eight new classrooms, a moot courtroom, and space for the dean's executive suite. At the south end of Stockton, meanwhile, the new Jacob Burns Law Library was already in use. A *Washington Post* architecture critic dubbed the ensemble "the most progressive piece of architecture and urban design commissioned by GW since the building boom began there a decade ago." To some, such flattery seemed a bit qualified, but others might recall that Stockton Hall, now sandwiched north and south by $16 million worth of new architecture, had been the second building erected on the G Street campus back in 1925.

In 1994, the law school campus received another edifice—the old president's house at 2003 G St. The building housed the law school admission offices and the *Environmental Lawyer*. Across the street, at 2000 G Street, was a town-house that served as the headquarters for GW's legal clinics. Two doors down, another townhouse served as the headquarters for GW's law review. Students also benefited from renovated and spectacularly comfortable lounges in which to study and from an increased number of study spaces in the library. The law school had become a well-appointed place.

Although scholarly pre-eminence may excite less notice than flashy clinical programs, the National Law Center so dominates certain specialized fields that GW has become, for many aspiring attorneys, their school of choice. Its law program in government procurement, for example, is one of a kind and, not surprisingly, given the National Law Center's Washington location, constitutes one of the center's four major degree programs. Co-directed by Frederick Lees and Joshua Schwartz, the program has its own mini-center, which publishes standard works for teaching and reference in the government procurement field.

Not unique, but certainly one of the first, Professor Arnold Rietze's environmental law program is now in its 25th year. Rietze, who joined the faculty in 1967 and whose research focuses on the legal means of dealing with polluted air, water, and hazardous waste, has been credited with creating at GW one of the most comprehensive environmental law programs in the country; it attracts some of the best-qualified students in the field.

Also bidding for the nation's "most comprehensive" is the National Law Center's program in international and comparative law. Headed by Thomas Buergenthal, former dean of American University's law school, the program offers more than 20 courses in the field. Buergenthal, who joined the law faculty in 1967, holds the Lobingier professorship. A Holocaust survivor, he has been a prominent writer and advocate for the protection of international human rights. As an activist, he served as a judge and later as president of the Inter-American Court of Human Rights. He was also a member of the Truth Commission on El Salvador. The program he heads encourages students to exploit the abundance of professional opportunities that beckon them from dozens of nearby international agencies.

The Intellectual Property Law Program, the National Law Center's fourth major program, is the nation's largest. It can claim ancestry from a single class in patent law first taught at GW in 1891 by the commissioner of patents. Today, because protecting intellectual property is no longer just a matter of domestic concern, its director, Harold Wegner, routinely places students in overseas research positions and is himself active in United Nations' efforts to create a model global patent law.

Among more than 60 full-time faculty, three are former law school deans and six hold endowed professorships. Jerome Barron, who fits both categories, is a national authority on First Amendment law and, in company with fellow law professor Thomas Dienes, publishes widely in the fields of civil rights and constitutional law. Thomas Morgan, former dean of Emory Law School and one-time president of the Association of American Law Schools, holds a professorship in anti-trust law and has published a widely used casebook in professional responsibility. Professors William Painter, David Seidelson, and Stephen Saltzburg hold other endowed professorships. Saltzburg also runs the center's trial advocacy program.

Specialists, many of whose casebooks are required reading for law students around the country, include David Sharpe (admiralty law), Leroy Merrifield and Charles Craver (labor law), Lewis Solomon (corporations, trusts, and federal taxation), Andrew Spanogle (consumer protection), Peter Raven-Hansen (national security law), and Ira Lupu, who publishes on legal issues relating to the religious establishment. The National Law Center's present dean, Jack Friedenthal, is well known for treatises on evidence and civil procedure. For live audiences beyond the classroom, Professor Mary Cheh projects the familiar presence of a regular commentator on national public television and radio, and James Starrs appears in the media whenever controversial forensic evidence comes under public scrutiny.

Because distinction has a price tag, the center owes much to the generosity of its alumni. Jacob Burns, LL.B. '24, LL.D. '70, who was a wealthy New York attorney, over the years gave more than $7 million to his alma mater. A former trustee of the University, he was long active in law school affairs. The Jacob Burns Law Library now houses a research collection of approximately 400,000 volumes.

Other benefactors include Lyle and Freda Alverson, whose bequest of $7.5 million, arriving in 1986, provided

Professor Stephen A. Saltzburg makes use of the National Law Center's Moot Courtroom for his trial advocacy class.

A GW law school family. GW trustee Sheldon Cohen, B.A. '50, J.D. '52, (center) with his daughters (left) Sharon Cohen, J.D. '90, and Laura Cohen Apelbaum, J.D. '84. Sharon's husband, Michael Liebman, is also a law school alumnus (J.D. '89).

enough endowment to fund three junior faculty positions and four endowed chairs. Following his graduation in 1918, Lyle Alverson joined other young idealists, like William C. Bullitt and John Foster Dulles, to make up part of Woodrow Wilson's entourage during the Paris peace negotiations. Subsequently, Alverson prospered in the investment business in New York, and for many years during his retirement, headed the Sun Coast chapter of the GW law school alumni association.

The Class of 1950 produced another generous benefactor in the person of Theodore Lerner, whose career as a real estate developer in suburban Maryland and Virginia produced the gift that built Lerner Hall. Dedicated in 1984, it was the center's first new classroom building to be erected on campus since the completion of Stockton Hall nearly a half century earlier.

AN OBSESSION WITH RATINGS

Practicing attorneys are supposed to be competitive, but perhaps no less so than law schools' preoccupation with where they rank with respect to rivals.

Sometimes they just have to settle for being "among" the "best." Here are some samplings in GW's favor:

1900: GW draws prestige from becoming a charter member of the American Association of Law Schools.

1933: GW law school is rated as Class A by the Council on Legal Education of the American Bar Association, putting it in company with those of Harvard, Yale, Columbia, and Michigan. (GW is still admitting persons with two years of college, but boasts that 60 percent have B.A.s.)

1978: A survey by the *National Law Journal* places GW 14th nationwide, a ranking based on selectivity. Only 21.69 percent of its applicants are admitted.

1983: GW law graduates are ranked "superior" in a survey conducted by University of Florida Law Professor Scott Van Alstyne, who used such criteria as selective admissions, college grades, standardized test scores, faculty salaries, and funding. (Van Alstyne tried to have the last word. He gave the

"superior" rating to graduates of 36 schools, but dismissed the idea that schools could be ranked "like a magic...top-10 football poll." Taken as a group, he wrote, the top 36 "all produce superior lawyers.")

1987: National Law Center graduates outdistance all others—including those from Georgetown, American, and Harvard—in passing the Maryland Bar Exam (an 87 percent pass rate).

1990: *U.S. News and World Report* gives the NLC it highest rating ever—23rd in a national survey comparing reputation, selectivity, placement, and instructional resources. (Dean Jack Friedenthal's deanly reaction: "I'm pleased, but I'm not satisfied...We stand weak [in the listing] on resources.")

However outsiders may compare its standing with others, the National Law Center can look with pride at what it has done for itself. In the past 30 years, the number of applications has increased tenfold; and of those admitted, the level of percentile in the Law School Admission Test has risen from 45 to 90.

CHANGING STANDARDS: A RETROSPECTIVE

As has been suggested, concerns about financial resources—both those of the school and those of its students—have mingled with worries about meeting national standards. When the school first opened in 1865, evening classes were the rule, and standards were minimal. To earn a Bachelor of Laws degree, students attended hour-long evening classes three times a week. By 1950, a three-year curriculum had become the norm. Full-time day students now spent 14 hours a week in class for six semes-

ters; part-time evening students took 10 hours a week for eight semesters. These norms, here and elsewhere, reflected a country-wide tightening of standards that began in the 1950s, and went on for two decades. Upgrading also put an end to a good many unaccredited institutions. Here in the District in 1954, the GW law school took over the National Law School, while American University absorbed the Washington College of Law. By 1970, the American Bar Association and the American Association of Law Schools reported they had very nearly achieved their goal of nationwide standardization. Critics, however, claimed the result had been to produce a large number of second-level schools with fewer elite institutions.

Associate Justice of the U.S. Supreme Court Ruth Bader Ginsburg came to campus in 1994 to speak to the law students as part of the National Law Center's Enrichment Program.

CHANGES OF VENUE

Rather than try to incorporate each relocation of the law school into the text, we offer a simple listing of its successive sites:

1865-84: The Columbian Law Building on 5th Street between D and E Streets in the Old Trinity Church facing Judiciary Square;

1884-1899: The first floor of the Columbian University Building at 15th and H Streets where the law lecture hall could seat 500;

1899-1910: A three-story structure adjoining the University Building on H Street;

1910-1921: Two upper floors of the Masonic Temple at the intersection of New York Avenue, 13th and H Streets;

1921-1925: A remodeled, four-story building formerly owned by the Justice Department, on K Street facing McPherson Square where its classrooms accommodated 1,000 students;

1925-1984: Stockton Hall on 20th Street between G and H; and

1984 to the present: Stockton and Lerner Halls, and the Burns Law Library.

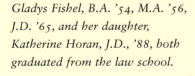

Gladys Fishel, B.A. '54, M.A. '56, J.D. '65, and her daughter, Katherine Horan, J.D., '88, both graduated from the law school.

The HATCHET

The George Washington University — Washington, D.C.

Wednesday, May 6,

Volume 66, No. 49

GW STRIKE LEADERS raise their fists in silent tribute to the five Kent State students killed Monday. The massive rally at the Center, held to protest the shootings, broke up with hundreds of striking students streaming to classrooms.

Much of the school shut down within 30 mi cancelled classes for the remainder of the

GW SHUT DO

by Jon Higman
Managing Editor

CLASSES HAVE BEEN cancelled by University President Lloyd H. Elliott as the first effective student strike in GW history cut average class attendance to below 30%.

"Let us hope that reason, judgment and restraint will guide each one of us in this troubled time," Elliott asked.

Meanwhile, strike demonstrations grow progressively larger as hundreds of students turned out at GW and other area campuses to stop "business as usual" in protest against the American system.

The nationwide boycott, which has closed scores of American universities, has accumulated issues in the past week. But organizers see all of them — the American troops in Indochina, the Black Panthers in jail in Connecticut and the National Guardsmen in Ohio — as interrelated expressions of the government they challenge.

Highlight of the two days of demonstrations was yesterday's solemn procession through campus by over 700 students marching to mourn the five students shot dead at Kent State and to gather support for the strike here.

After walking silently down GW's sidewalks, the group, swollen to over 1,000, gathered to rededicate the University Center in memory of their fellow students slain the day before.

Between chants of "On strike! Shut it down!" the crowd approved renaming the building the "Kent State al Center."

then broke up into small groups to pus to persuade the profes x minds and support

severely. Othe much affecte

Strike lea into final e during nex remain h schedule

The C organiz of the the st

T
or
a
s

National Protest
Focuses on GW

by Jack Levine
Hatchet Staff Writer

the not so peaceful eye of the
Saturday's planned

University officials later

photo by Lampke

WN

sroom buildings, however, were not

are calling for extension of the strike
There will almost certainly be activity
x's reading period, since feelings should
hrough the nationally-planned rallies
.C. this weekend.
mpus has been proclaimed the center for
e weekend's actions, much to the dismay
administration and the surprise of much of
body.
in accord with the promptings of veteran
Rennie Davis, who, in a speech here Monday
, noted that the University is "the most
ally located university in the world," with the
House less than half a mile away.

Monday Extra

atchet Schedule
THE HATCHET'S Thursday edition has
en pushed up to today because of the strike
and cancellation of classes. Because of the
weekend march on Washington, we will
abandon our original production schedule,
ich called for our final issue to hit the
orrow.

Idealism
and Activism

(Above) Cheerleader Dianne Lerner helps in the demolition of the old buildings on the site of the new university center during initial groundbreaking ceremonies in November 1966.

(Right) Jacob Burns, LL.B. '24, LL.D. '70, alumnus and benefactor to the National Law Center.

(Far right) From his Rice Hall balcony, GW President Lloyd Elliott had a good view of the construction work on the new university center, 1968.

CONSTRUCTION BOOM

If Elliott had a core project at GW, it was the physical expansion of the University. He quickly gained the trustees' approval for the master plan that had begun to take shape during Carroll's presidency. GW became more aggressive about acquiring property in the Foggy Bottom area. By 1988, this property was valued at $100 million and constituted at least half of the University's total endowment. By way of contrast, the endowment totaled less than $9 million at the beginning of Elliott's presidency.

GW used a fund-raising strategy that was well suited to its urban environment. It would acquire property and turn some of it into much-needed University facilities. Other properties would be rented for commercial purposes with the money used to fund building and other projects on campus.

Not since the 1930s had GW seen so much construction on its campus. The first structure of many finished in the Elliott era was the Jacob Burns Law Library, completed in 1967. The law school held a special place in Lloyd Elliott's affections. Throughout his presidency, Elliott retained a special pride in its accomplishments. He described the National Law Center as "one of the foremost in quality." He noted that, as in so many things, the Washington location contributed to the law school's success. For example, at GW, one could engage in the first-hand, clinical study of administrative and constitutional law.

Another central project of the Elliott era was what one University administrator described as the "internationalization" of the University. The president's interest in international affairs was apparent early in his administration. In March 1966, he decided to create two new schools. One would be called the School of Government and Business Administration, a direct offshoot of the School of Government that had been established in 1928 with a $1 million endowment from the Supreme Council 33rd degree of the Scottish Rite Freemasonry, Southern Jurisdiction. The other school would be called the School of Public and International Affairs; it is known today as the Elliott School of International Affairs, in tribute to the president's role in starting and nurturing it.

In announcing the change, Lloyd Elliott made a typically low-key announcement. He talked about the "continued growth and development of programs in these fields" that brought more than 900 graduate students to Washington each year and that required the services of more than 70 faculty members. In fact, however, Elliott took a keen interest in international affairs and saw foreign students as an important addition to the GW student body. The School of Public and International Affairs became the new home of the Sino-Soviet Institute. It also housed the international affairs programs

offered at the various war colleges. The School of Government and Business Administration, meanwhile, sharpened its focus on public administration and business management.

In a further move to rationalize the structure of GW's graduate programs, the trustees voted on July 1, 1967, to establish a separate Graduate School of Arts and Sciences. That was, in effect, the graduate branch of the Columbian College, one that offered degrees in typical academic fields such as history and physics.

The history department, with such able scholars as Roderic Davison and Lois Schwoerer, had, with little fanfare, developed a national reputation for scholarship and teaching. This reputation stretched back to the days when GW historian Samuel Flagg Bemis won the 1927 Pulitzer Prize for his book on Pinckney's Treaty. The Graduate School of Arts and Sciences allowed the history department, and other similarly excellent GW departments, to achieve more visibility.

THE DEATH OF FOOTBALL

It was not so much the creation of the new schools as the destruction of the football program that attracted student attention. The move to end football at GW began in 1965 when the Faculty Senate voted in favor of discontinuing the sport. The faculty preferred to spend the football team's annual $250,000 price-tag elsewhere. *The Hatchet* sided with the faculty, arguing that the team was mediocre,

In 58 years of varsity competition, GW was noted more for good sportsmanship than for winning seasons.

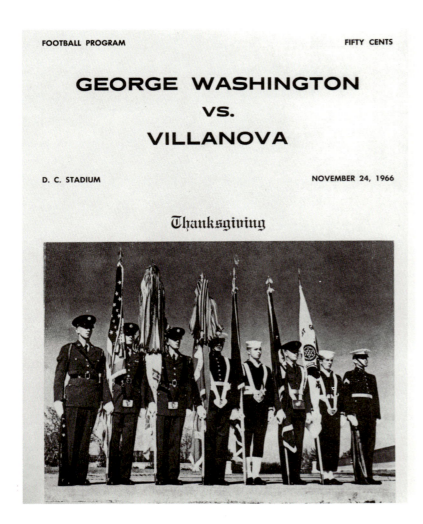

(Left) Program from GW's last football game, played against Villanova in November 1966.

the crowds were small, and the support was negligible. The Student Council strongly favored continuing the program. President Elliott kept his own counsel, and the trustees voted to continue the program.

In 1966, GW suffered another losing season in football, winning four, but losing six. Since the University had joined the Southern Conference in 1941, it had compiled a losing record. Indeed, in 58 years of varsity competition, GW had lost far more than half of its games. Elliott, although attached to the idea of intercollegiate athletics, began to think in a disciplined way about ending the football program. He told the trustees in October that the University had to do something, "and the sooner, the better," to take the students off the street corners of Foggy Bottom and give them some physical exercise.

GW, unlike suburban schools, had a singular lack of playing fields and open spaces where one could play catch or a game of touch football. Elliott wanted to build a new athletic and recreation facility that would, at long last, replace the Tin Tabernacle and provide a real venue for student recreation. As a not-incidental benefit, the basketball team could play its games on the GW campus, rather than using such remote locations as Fort Myer as its home court.

In Elliott's mind, the issues of ending football and building a new gym became linked. The money saved from football would help to fund the new facility. Football, he hinted, might have to go, and he offered to send the trustees a complete report in January 1967.

Jim Camp, GW's football coach who had been voted the Southern Conference's coach of the year, got wind of Elliott's plans and on December 19 announced his decision to quit. "Red" Auerbach, the Celtics coach, had begun to lose faith in the University's ability to field competitive teams in any sport. Traveling about the country, he said he was ashamed to tell people that GW had "no field houses, no football field on which to practice. They don't believe me."

In this atmosphere, Elliott wrote his report to the trustees. He decided that, although the students wanted to keep football, it was not a unifying activity for the student body. Attendance at D.C. Stadium (later RFK Stadium) for the games never exceeded 15,000. Average attendance was on the order of 4,200 in a stadium that seated 49,000. Perhaps 1,000 GW undergraduates attended a typical game, even though upperclassmen claimed that they went to nearly all of the team's home games. Furthermore, the Redskins had established themselves as the town's premiere sports attraction, and their games could be seen free of charge on television. It was the D.C. trend, one followed at Georgetown, Catholic, and American, to disband football programs. In a memo to the trustees dated January 12, 1967, Elliott urged GW to follow suit and to save the millions

of dollars that a football team would cost in the future. The trustees concurred. The last game that GW ever played was against Villanova, and it was a loss.

The Hatchet, as might be expected, took the news in stride. The major concerns of the editors centered not so much on football as on the announced decision to publish twice a week. The paper, perhaps the most important source of communication on campus, would now appear on Mondays and Thursdays.

President Elliott, for his part, concentrated on the building campaign. Groundbreaking for a new student center had taken place in November 1966, during homecoming weekend of the last football season. Elliott said that the center represented a milestone in what he described as "the chain of necessary events in the University's transition from a commuter to a residential institution." The student center, along with the proposed new athletic center and library, would provide solid facilities for the conduct of the University's scholastic and extracurricular life.

GW AND THE STUDENT UPRISINGS

Despite this evidence of progress, GW soon entered an era of confrontation between students and administrators that would absorb much of Lloyd Elliott's energy and delay the initiation of important academic projects. The catalysts, at GW as at many campuses, were the Vietnam War and the arrival, in record numbers, of members of the postwar "baby boom" generation. By 1972, the era of traditional student life that had begun in the Marvin era was over.

As late as the fall of 1967, the Vietnam War remained a peripheral issue at GW. The chief difference between GW and other universities was its location. At other universities, opponents of the war urged mass action against the war that involved large demonstrations in Washington. GW was already in Washington. It was the closest university in America to the centers of national power. Hence, whatever the views of its students, GW became an important staging ground for protests against the war. As the saying went, it served as the "Holiday Inn of the Revolution."

The late 1960s were a time of protest for the nation, and especially for GW—located in the nation's capital. Student disturbances often found their way to the steps of Rice Hall—home of GW's administrative offices, including the President's Office.

In October 1967, the University held a teach-in on the Vietnam War that marked the prelude to the March on the Pentagon, which took place the next day. As many as 200 GW students were among the 50,000 protestors who attended a rally at the Lincoln Memorial and marched to the Pentagon. Earlier that week, in what would become a familiar pattern, a small group of students, who happened to be from colleges around Ithaca, New York, used GW as the launching point for their march to the 23rd Street entrance of the State Department. There they sat-in until educator Paul Goodman, who was speaking inside, was allowed to talk to the group.

Martin Luther King's assassination brought the issue of civil rights to the forefront of campus politics.

At this point, the campus was about equally divided on the war. Slightly more than 49.5 percent of students surveyed in an informal poll said that the United States should not participate in the war. Nearly 46.5 percent of the students polled defended the United States's role in the conflict.

THE CAMPUS AND BLACK EQUALITY

Concern over the war soon shaded into feelings of despair over racial inequality in Washington, D.C. When major riots occurred in the District after Martin Luther King's assassination, the civil rights issue became a focal point of campus politics. "The white man just can't understand what we're complaining about," said one black man on campus. "Look at GW. How can a University with such a plantation attitude exist in a city that is over 65 percent black?"

Concern over the treatment of blacks on campus and over the place of black cultural concerns in the curriculum culminated on April 26, 1968, in a protest march of more than 200 students to the steps of Rice Hall, home of GW's high-level administrative offices. The students marched in support of demands made earlier by the Black Students Union. These included black-oriented courses, better job benefits for black staff members, stricter enforcement of open membership policies in GW student clubs and social groups, stronger links between the campus and the rest of the District, and a policy of not doing business with firms that failed to obey the terms of the 1964 Civil Rights Act.

The presence of the demonstrators brought Vice President for Student Affairs William P. Smith to the Rice Hall steps. He announced that the University would comply with the demands. The history department, he reported, had already decided to add a course in black history. He assured the crowd that the University was "committed to doing everything in its power to strengthen its thrust as an institution in this community and with all disadvantaged groups." Later Smith admitted to being haunted by the fires which had blanketed the city after Martin Luther King's death. "I couldn't escape the fact that I've been part of this failure," he said.

If Vice President Smith experienced a moment of epiphany, many GW students remained unmoved by the 1968 riots and their campus aftermath. Asked about the new courses in black history, one student said, "I don't really care. No one's gonna take them."

Other GW undergraduates proved this student wrong. In 1968, the University hired J. Saunders Redding as a professor of American history and civilization. Redding was a leader among the nation's black intellectuals, an inspiration for the "new black intellectuals" who would be acclaimed in the 1990s. Redding had previously taught at the Hampton Institute, a historically black school of national renown, and directed the Division of Research and Publications for the National Endowment for the Humanities.

Continued on p. 114

The Elliott School

The Elliott School's first incarnation, impressively named the School of Comparative Jurisprudence and Diplomacy, owed its origins not to a political science department (not yet invented) but to the law school. As its name suggests, "international affairs" then meant plying students with heavy doses of international law, a smattering of current world affairs, and treating them to the comparative merits of various legal concepts evolved since the days of Hammurabi.

Launched with considerable fanfare (President William McKinley and his cabinet attended its birthing), the School of Comparative Jurisprudence and Diplomacy began with 90 students and 11 faculty—and lasted only six years. It proved to be one of President Charles Needham's ill-fated extravagances.

With enrollments in steep decline by 1904, President Needham cut his losses. He put "jurisprudence" back in the law school and tucked what was left of the school's curriculum into a reshuffled and newly named unit.

The second embodiment of international affairs fared no better than the first. Needham's insistence that the School of Politics and Diplomacy offer only advanced degrees made short work of it. With something akin to sleight of hand, Needham arranged for politics and diplomacy's sudden death and instant resurrection in 1907 as the College of the Political Sciences—GW's third way station for students casting about for an international affairs curriculum.

(Above) Admiral Charles Stockton rebuilt a financially distressed university.

(Below) A 1920's Columbian University classroom.

A pre-information-age classroom.

Like its two predecessors, the College of the Political Sciences lived a parasitic existence, with faculty (and now students) borrowed from the liberal arts college. Between 1907 and 1913, some 12 Columbian departments contributed faculty, among them what might be called the "big three" of all international affairs curricula: history, economics, and political science.

The combination was right, but the cash flow was bad. For some reason, large numbers of undergraduates, while paying their tuition to Columbian College, were allowed to take courses in the College of the Political Sciences without any payback from Columbian. This tuition deficit, plus the Panic of 1907, plus Charles Needham's notorious book-

keeping, added up to financial disaster. Not even the succession of economists who served as its deans could save the college from an early demise. In 1911, the redoubtable Admiral Charles H. Stockton (Needham's successor) observed unhappily that the College of the Political Sciences "will never be self-supporting." Two years later, he cited "a lapse of subscriptions" as reason enough to close it down. In 1913, international affairs programs took refuge in Columbian College.

Within the college, the international affairs program lived briefly as a separate Department of International Law and Diplomacy, only to be incorporated into the political science department in 1914.

Roderick S. French, vice president for academic affairs, left his fingerprints on many notable University achievements, but nowhere else did he work so effectively (often behind the scenes) to accomplish so visible a result as he did—teamed with Dean "Mickey" East—in creating the independent self-standing school of international affairs we know today.

In 1928, President Cloyd Heck Marvin created the School of Government. Born in the high era of government-business cooperation, the new school was Marvin's logical extension of the Coolidge dictum that if "the business of America is business," America's business overseas should require an understanding of international relations. This logic meant combining "policy-oriented" historians, economists, and political scientists with the "more professionally oriented" faculty who taught classes in commerce, business administration, and finance.

That these somewhat disparate faculties managed to cooperate for 38 years can be ascribed in part to the million-dollar endowment President Marvin secured from the Scottish Rite Masons in 1928. The "Masonic connection," while not overtly anti-Catholic, reflected the lodge's subliminal concern that Georgetown's School of Foreign Service needed a non-sectarian competitor—a concern reflected in the Masons' condition that

should GW "cease to be a non-sectarian institution," the million dollar gift would revert. During the next 60 years, some 870 GW students of "government" would benefit from Scottish Rite and Wolcott fellowships.

The international affairs-related faculty—earlier referred to as the "big three"—never felt quite comfortable in affiliation with their "professional" colleagues in the School of Government.

In October 1960, the School of Government became the School of Government, Business, and International Affairs. The change was not entirely cosmetic. At the same time, "public and international affairs," in acquiring its own assistant dean, seemed to have reached at least a half-way house along the road to independence.

It took Lloyd Elliott to go the rest of the way. On January 20, 1966, a month before his inaugural convocation, the 14th president reminded the trustees that three years earlier they had given his predecessor discretionary authority

to split the school into its component parts. Elliott said he saw no reason not to "carry out this authority." The time was right, he said: both the international affairs and business school programs were well developed and could stand by themselves.

Near the end of the spring semester, the two faculties, after 38 years of troubled wedlock, celebrated their divorce at a festive dinner held in the Roger Smith Hotel. GW's institutional evolution had finally produced a School of Public and International Affairs.

The school's first dean was quiet, courtly 62-year-old Hiram Stout, a scholar who had published modestly some 30 years earlier and was soon to retire. Today, the Elliott School and its research institutes have 28 budgeted faculty and 1,600 students, supported by a full-time staff of 25 persons. It's home to a range of special programs and student services that Hiram Stout could not have dreamed of.

President Elliott's successor, Stephen Joel Trachtenberg, has given the Elliott School of International Affairs his unflagging support. He most recently dedicated the whole of Stuart Hall to the Elliott School. Trachtenberg is shown here at his first opening convocation in 1989 with international affairs student Brian Hengen.

Building what today is the Elliott School needed leaders at the top who possessed not only vision but a willingness to commit resources. Those resources, as the second dean of the School of Public and International Affairs discovered, would not be forthcoming—not during his deanship. That the school remained so long neglected, however, can scarcely be laid at the door of Burton Sapin. Year after year, during his deanship from 1969 to 1983, Sapin boldly created new multidisciplinary programs: Russian studies (1970); science, technology and public policy (1971); Latin American studies (1972); and urban affairs (1973). During the Sapin era, the school's on-campus programs multiplied and flourished.

Forces for upscaling the school began to gather shortly after Burt Sapin retired in 1983. While History Professor Peter Hill, as acting dean, praised the well-structured programs Sapin had left behind, he was sharply critical of the school's "weak deanship, dubious faculty structure, [and] curricular diffuseness." In fact, changes were already in prospect. By the spring of 1985, President Elliott's hardworking Commission for the Year 2000 had laid out one of the University's major and lasting objectives: to capitalize on the "international" status that the city and, therefore, the University should reflect.

Everything needed to make the Elliott School (so named in 1989) the flourishing institution it is today happened in the late 1980s. From 1985 on, the new dean, Maurice A. East, not known for his reticence, proceeded without stint to tell "Rice Hall" what he needed. He was

seldom refused. Resources poured into the Elliott School as never before. But the outpouring came not without support from East's key collaborator, the Vice President for Academic Affairs. Roderick French has left his fingerprints on many notable University achievements: experimental programs, the Northern Virginia campus, equal opportunity programs for women and minorities, and minority hirings. The list is almost endless, but nowhere else did he work so effectively (often behind the scenes) to accomplish so visible a result as he did in creating, teamed with "Mickey" East, the independent, self-standing school of international affairs we know today.

During the East era, the school's number of fully budgeted faculty grew to 24; freshmen and sophomores who once came to the school via Columbian College in their junior year were now admitted directly to its programs.

In token of its new directions, the University also committed additional funds to two of the school's research entities: the new Space Policy Center, headed by John Logsdon, a preeminent figure in the field, and to that venerable relic of the cold war, the Institute for Sino-Soviet Studies (since renamed the Institute for European, Russian, and Eurasian Studies). When James Millar arrived to head the institute in September 1989, he helped to make it one of the best in the nation.

Emerging from the collection of disparate programs inherited by Hiram Stout in 1966, the Elliott School today stands as a premier institution in its field, as selective in its graduate admissions as any, but the most exalted of its rivals.

Moreover, in putting markers along the University's chosen road to "internationalization," the school has had the unflagging support of Elliott's successor, Stephen Joel Trachtenberg, whose achievement it has been to make the school a thing of substance. In aid of that commitment, the new president enlisted the generosity of Dorothy Shapiro and the other trustees of the J. B. and Maurice C. Shapiro Charitable Trust to provide the school with graduate fellowships and an endowed chair. And most recently, he dedicated the whole of Stuart Hall to the Elliott School and authorized the building's renovation in time for GW's 175th celebration.

Continued from p. 108

Born in Wilmington, Delaware, he had studied at Brown University, where he was a member of Phi Beta Kappa. Between 1953 and 1963, he served on the board of editors of *The American Scholar*, the prestigious Phi Beta Kappa publication. A prolific writer, Redding's books included *To Make a Poet Black, No Day of Triumph*, and *They Came in Chains*. This eminent scholar proceeded to breathe life into black studies at GW.

To be sure, Redding and the other GW faculty members taught their courses in interesting times. One GW graduate student, who assisted Redding, recalled that both factions of a split Students for a Democratic Society (SDS) enrolled in Redding's class one fall and proceeded to "dominate the class with their high decibel disputes with one another over the heads of the rest of the class." Redding, in the contemporary idiom, kept his cool, and the graduate student concluded that in retrospect the students' intrusions were "creative and constructive."

Redding's endeavors smoothed the path for black studies courses to be offered in other GW departments and schools. Begun on the undergraduate level, black history soon entered the graduate curriculum. Letitia Woods Brown, Redding's successor, proved to be a dynamic historian of the African-American urban experience. And James Horton, Brown's successor and still an active member of the GW faculty, has received recognition as one of the best teachers on campus. Horton's work on antebellum black communities, which has done much to illuminate previously neglected aspects of the black experience, has attracted considerable notice within the history profession.

The civil rights revolution had repercussions at GW that extended well beyond the classrooms of Redding. Students debated the issues on and off the campus. Some of the discussions took place in the group homes, which some called communes, that stretched from the campus to Dupont Circle. Others occurred in the tiny headquarters of the United Christian Fellowship where Mal Davis, the anything but reverent chaplain, hosted all manner of radical gatherings with bluff good humor and boundless tolerance.

In the spring of 1968, members of the student government debated the Human Relations Act, which was intended to enforce non-discrimination in campus organizations. When passed on May 10, 1968, it required recognized campus organizations to "have a provision in their constitution or bylaws that membership shall not be restricted on the basis of race, religion, or national origin." The act also established a student court to enforce the law.

CIVIL RIGHTS AND CAMPUS SOCIAL LIFE

The Human Relations Act profoundly altered the fraternity and sorority system at GW. Although no fraternities were found to be in violation of the act, many sororities were. The national by-laws of

these sororities contained provisions that explicitly discriminated against members of certain ethnic groups. Differences between the local chapter at George Washington, under a mandate to comply with the Human Relations Act, and the national organization caused some GW sororities to cease operations.

On September 23, 1968, Kappa Delta became the first of the GW sororities to go out of business. In February of 1969, Alpha Delta Pi and Zeta Tau Alpha also gave up their active status. By 1971, 10 of the 14 GW sororities had closed. Four of 12 fraternities ceased operations by 1971, in part because the entire Greek system was breaking down.

As a result of the decline of the Greek system, the character of social life on campus changed. No longer did events like Greek Week, Greek Sing, Prom, and Derby Day dominate GW's social calendar. By 1971, much more of the campus life was organized by residents of the various dormitories. Informal and ad hoc events predominated.

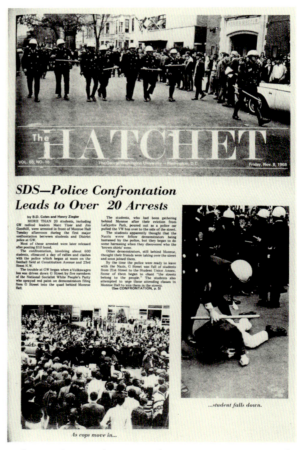

(Above) The Hatchet covered news of campus protests. This issue featured a story about the arrest of 20 students following a confrontation between about 600 students and the District of Columbia police. According to the article, "The trouble at GW began when a Volkswagen bus was driven down G Street by five members of the National Socialist White People's Party who sprayed red paint on demonstrators filing from G Street into the Quad behind Monroe Hall."

(Left) GW during the 1960s and 1970s became an important staging ground for protests, earning the University the nickname, "Holiday Inn of the Revolution." Shown here, Strike Day at Lafayette Park, May 5, 1970.

The University itself sponsored far fewer dances and mixers. The homecoming dance, held at a downtown hotel with the participants in formal dress, attracted fewer and fewer participants. The event suffered both from the elimination of the football program and a general sense of apathy: it appeared to be a relic from a different era. Indeed, social rituals took on a whole different meaning in a time in which, as *The Hatchet* put it, "arranging to have a guest of the opposite sex spend the night in a dorm is a mere formality."

In 1969, a sportswriter at *The Hatchet* wrote an editorial that caught another important dimension of the changes at GW. He urged the school to leave the Southern Conference because, as he argued, "GW is no longer a southern school." Both in student body and viewpoint it was a northern school in which over 80 percent of the students came from the northeastern part of the country. When GW looked beyond Washington for ideas and inspiration, it turned north rather than south.

1968

The academic year that began in September 1968 marked the real start of student protest at George Washington. The confrontations started even before the first day of classes. Mark Tizer, a self-described student radical, interrupted a freshman book discussion session, urging the new students to consider texts beyond those assigned in the classroom and to take an active role in opposition to the Vietnam War.

On September 30, a group of 100 students refused to leave the formal lounge of Thurston Hall after campus guards tried to enforce a midnight curfew. This incident had an entirely different feel from the G Street riots at the beginning of the decade. It began when a group of close to 100 students, both male and female, who had been attending a political meeting, left the basement of the Concordia Church and marched to Thurston Hall, still an all-women's dormitory. They announced their intention to use the lounge for a love-in and put up a sign that declared "this lounge has been liberated." Shelly Green, the president of the dorm, then asked the members of the group to leave since they were violating University rules that forbade non-residents and males to remain in the dorm after midnight. In the end, the University called upon Metropolitan Police to force the protestors to leave.

On the one hand, the dispute concerned GW's right to enforce parietal rules on dormitory residents, and in that sense it was a very traditional form of student protest. On the other hand, the incident lacked the playful tone of earlier fraternity stunts. It was a much more direct challenge to authority.

On October 1, 1968, Dave Dellinger and Rennie Davis, nationally known leaders of SDS, addressed an anti-war rally in the Yard behind Lisner Hall. Close to 2,000 students gathered to hear the speeches, a far larger crowd than for previous political events. At

"Trial" of Students for a Democratic Society (SDS) after their occupation of Maury Hall, 1969.

one point a fight broke out between a group carrying a Viet Cong flag and a group of GW fraternity members. To counter the Viet Cong flag, several GW students lowered an American flag out of the library windows overlooking the rally.

The speeches and protests continued as wave after wave of political action groups came to Washington. On October 17, Mark Rudd, the ex-Columbia student who had figured prominently in spring 1968 protests at Columbia University that ended in direct confrontations with the New York City police, spoke at GW. "Students are completely disgusted with what our universities are being used for," he said. Two days later, a handful of SDS members staged a demonstration outside of the GW Board of Trustees meetings at Airlie House in Virginia. They demanded that J. Edgar Hoover be removed from the Board of Trustees and that there be greater student participation in decision making at GW.

Faculty tried to steer these conversations into what they perceived to be constructive channels. As often as seemed necessary, and particularly at those intense moments when National Guardsmen were ready to drive demonstrators from the Mall to the campus, Robert A. Jones, Harry Yeide, or John Morgan worked the edges of volatile gatherings in the Yard. They engaged students in debate, cautioned them against actions that might get them arrested, and helped to staff a faculty-student "communications center" in what is now the Alumni House.

As the students pushed their demands, often using the University as the stage from which to broadcast their views, the nation prepared to elect Richard Nixon as president of the United States. An election day protest took place in Lafayette Park across from the White House and resulted in 80 arrests. It soon spilled over to the GW campus. About 75 D.C. riot police chased the protestors back to the campus and then occupied the campus for four hours.

The crowd that gathered between Monroe Hall and the Hall of Government taunted the police and pelted them with tomatoes. In response, the police waded into the crowd, swinging their night sticks freely and injuring some of the students. Three campus radical leaders were arrested in the election day riots, including Nick Greer, the head of the GW branch of SDS. The police cited Greer for jaywalking on his way to Lafayette Park. Then, according to *The Hatchet*, he was pushed into the street and dragged into a police van with a club pressed against his throat.

MAURY HALL

In the spring of 1969, a series of interrelated events involved nearly the entire campus in the protests over the Vietnam War. On the evening of April 23, a group of about 40 people, some of whom were members of the SDS chapter, seized and occupied the Institute

for Sino-Soviet Studies located in Maury Hall (since demolished). In the style of the sit-ins that had occurred at Harvard and Columbia, the group members barricaded the windows and doors with desks and chairs. In the front windows of the building, they hung posters of Trotsky, Mao Tse Tung, and Che Guevara, and they flew a red flag out of the central window.

In the idiom of the era, those who sat in at Maury Hall wanted to close down the war machine. They saw vital links between the war in Vietnam and the research that the University was undertaking for the military and the State Department. They demanded that the University eliminate the Sino-Soviet Institute, which they viewed as an ideological astringent that only inflamed cold war passions. They also wanted GW to cut all its ties with the military, including the Navy Logistics program, the Army Human Resources Research Office, and the ROTC programs. Lloyd Elliott later did exactly that, ending programs such as ROTC that had been on campus throughout the postwar era. Finally, the group linked its demands to those of the Black Students Union and called for open admissions for all blacks.

The siege lasted for about five hours before the protestors were removed by the police. For much of the evening, a group of GW students milled around the building. According to the campus newspaper, those outside of the building were mostly hostile toward those inside.

Within a few days, the faculty met in an emergency session in Lisner Auditorium to discuss the situation. Even though the faculty urged President Elliott only to call on the police as a "last resort," it gave the president an overwhelming vote of confidence. They passed a special resolution of approval for the administration's handling of the evacuation of Maury Hall. Some professors worried about the prospect of losing research results that had taken years to compile at the hands of students who occupied University offices. Even as the faculty met in Lisner Auditorium, a large group of students gathered in front of the auditorium debating the propriety of the Maury Hall takeover as an anti-war tactic. The bonds that held the University together were becoming frayed.

Nor did the incident end there. It dragged on for the remainder of the spring term and into the next fall. In these years, the spring confrontation between the administration and its students became almost as ritualized as the senior prom had been in earlier years. In general, the anti-war movement mixed social and political elements in ways unappreciated by those who would later write about it.

Students gather at the Marvin Center to declare that the building should be named the "Kent State Memorial Center," 1970.

In the case of the Maury Hall seizure, University authorities decided to suspend seven of the students involved and to expel two others. According to *The Hatchet*, a student-faculty hearing committee overruled the punishments, and the Columbian College formally dismissed its charges two months later. Another demonstration followed—an occupation of the lobby of Rice Hall on May 20. The University issued a restraining order. The protestors remained in the lobby past closing time and ultimately were arrested. Four of the students drew brief jail terms.

As if to symbolize that the times were changing, GW received news on April 28, 1969, that former president Cloyd Heck Marvin had died. The Marvin era was emphatically over. Some greeted the new era with a great deal of hope: students appeared to be more thoughtful and to have lost the docility that characterized their behavior in earlier eras. Others regarded the changes with dismay: the decorum of the University, which permitted free expression and a freedom of inquiry in a civilized environment, was being lost.

MORE DEBATE AND A STRIKE

Even as the debate over the meaning of the anti-war protests continued, the University continued to chip away at the set of common rules that had guided it in Marvin's time. In May of 1969, for example, the policy of allowing students only three cuts per semester was discontinued. In the matter of attending classes, as in so many other things, students were on their own.

The debate over campus protest extended from one end of town to the other. In the summer of 1969, the House Committee on Internal Security (formerly the House Committee on Un-American Activities) conducted hearings regarding the Students for a Democratic Society. Lloyd Elliott and Calvin Linton, the dean of Columbian College, both testified. Elliott condemned those bent on "disruption for disruption's sake." He expressed concern over GW's location in which "protestors are more likely to receive a national audience" and noted that the campus was attractive to "individuals and groups around the country as a rallying point or launching pad for national demonstrations and confrontations."

Far from being over, the anti-war protests and rallies reached a peak in the 1969-1970 academic year. As many as 4,000 GW students and like-minded faculty observed the October moratorium by gathering behind the library and joining perhaps 35,000 demonstrators in a candlelight procession around the White House. GW students were also among those who listened to Dr. Benjamin Spock speak and then marched to 17th and F Streets, practically on the University's doorstep, to participate in a peaceful demonstration at the Selective Service headquarters. Even more GW students took part in the November moratorium, which attracted hundreds of thousands of college students to Washington.

(Above) The spring of 1970 became known as the "strike semester." Demonstrators from across the nation came to GW demanding space to lodge during their Washington protest. Classes were canceled (for the first time since the Civil War), rumors spread of bomb threats if the campus did not shut down, and the U.S. Marshal's Office was called in to remove non-GW demonstrators from University buildings.

In the spring of 1970 came the invasion of Cambodia, the death of four Kent State students at the hands of the National Guard, and the closing of universities across the nation. University students proclaimed themselves on strike, and the spring term entered the realm of history as the "strike semester." GW followed the general pattern, although, as always, the University's location put it in the national spotlight.

Harold Bright, the University provost, later issued a report that sounded like an account of a military campaign. He said that the period of greatest activity began on Monday, May 4, with yet another rally behind Lisner Hall. Once again, national leaders spoke at the rally, calling for a student strike. Rennie Davis of the Chicago Seven, a group made famous by the anti-war rallies at the 1968 Democratic convention in Chicago, demanded University space for non-GW students who were expected to attend a May 9 rally behind the White House. Students picketed classes on Monday afternoon. That evening the George Washington Student Strike Committee received space in the student center and went into 24-hour operation.

Protestors at Lafayette Park on
May 5, 1970—Strike Day.

On Tuesday, the tempo of picketing increased. According to Bright, pickets began actively to disrupt classes after a silent march in memory of the Kent State students. Since "hit and run" tactics affected so many points and for fear that violence would escalate, President Elliott canceled classes for the remainder of the week. The students had succeeded in shutting the University down.

Even after the suspension of classes, tensions rose. Administrators such as Bright heard rumors that there were weapons in the residence halls and received bomb threats. If the University did not shut down completely and make all its facilities available to the strike committee, there would be violence. The University refused to accede to these threats. In response, a group occupied Monroe Hall and another building on G Street, bringing bedding taken from the storage areas of residence halls into the occupied buildings. The University, in the person of John Cantini, the assistant vice president and assistant treasurer, asked that the demonstrators leave the buildings. When the demonstrators refused, the University requested a temporary restraining order. The U.S. Marshal's Office posted this order on Thursday morning.

The rally at the Ellipse passed quietly. Later on that Saturday night, however, a group, containing at least a few GW students, burned several cars near the intersection of 21st and Eye. A group then broke into the Hall of Government and began to throw furniture out. University authorities requested that the Metropolitan Police Department clear the area. Using tear gas, the police accomplished this goal without causing major injuries. On May 11, relative quiet returned to the University, although officials estimated $30,000 in property loss as a result of the various demonstrations.

Some members of the student body thought the strike to be nothing less than heroic; President Elliott and Harold Bright found the events of the strike semester highly unsettling. *The Hatchet* reported that the strike "tore through the entire fabric of the University, like no other event ever has." The strike was "an impressive piece of mass action and unity," in which the GW strike committee helped to arrange food and lodging for demonstrators who arrived from across the nation.

President Elliott viewed the strike and other uprisings of the period as a war. "I want you to know," he told a trustee, "that my whole objective is to win the war...This chaos, this hell that's let loose on campus, has to end. I want this university to be around when it's over."

Elliott took as his major objective simply to survive. He felt that GW "was particularly vulnerable to violence, to property damage," because most of the big demonstrations took place in Washington, D.C. "We thought we were vulnerable because of our location," he said, noting "it was such an attraction for protestors from other parts of the country...to pick George Washington as a kind of bivouac area, a rallying place, a place to meet." Elliott claimed that students in Madison (the University of Wisconsin) and Berkeley (the University of California) received advice to come to the GW campus. In the resulting game of survival, "we wanted to make concessions, compromises, only to get us through the next crisis."

John Cantini had charge of the University's security forces in this period. Together with Elliott and Vice President for Student Affairs William P. Smith, Cantini decided to hire a chief security officer and to spend whatever it took to protect the campus. In 1967, they selected the retiring chief of the Secret Service Division of the White House for the post, and he hired a relatively large security force. Through this official, the University gained contacts with local police forces across the nation. As a result, Elliott claimed, "We knew how many bus loads of protestors were coming from New Haven. We knew when they were going to arrive. We knew when they were going to depart. The same thing with Berkeley and Madison." Elliott believed such measures were necessary because the student uprisings constituted a "threat to American life which had to be opposed." "We can't let the bastards win," Elliott told himself. And yet, annoyed and anguished by the student radicals and by the course of events, Elliott also managed to exploit some of the calls for change and use them for constructive purposes.

EXPANSION: THE MARVIN CENTER

Neither at GW nor at many other universities did "the bastards" win. Instead, the economic downturn of the 1970s and then the formal end of the Vietnam War dampened the fires of student enthusiasm. At GW, the building campaign continued apace. Despite the distractions of student protests and despite the very hard line that Elliott took on the question of student discipline, he remained devoted to the expansion of the University. During the early 1970s, one milestone followed another.

Dorothy Betts Marvin (widow of former GW President Cloyd Heck Marvin) is shown at left of her portrait with her brother, George Betts, during the dedication of the Dorothy Betts Marvin Theatre.

In the winter of 1970, the new student center opened for student use. Even before its formal dedication, it played a large role in University life. It served as the nerve center for the strike, and on May 5 students gathered there and declared that it should be named the Kent State Memorial Center.

As it turned out, the University had other plans. It wanted to link the naming of the student center with GW's fund-raising efforts and hoped to attract a donor who would make a large "naming gift" for the center. Elliott thought that 1971, the sesquicentennial of the University, would be an appropriate year to find such a donor and hold a dedication ceremony for the center.

One day, Dorothy Betts Marvin, the widow of former President Marvin, made an appointment to see Lloyd Elliott. Elliott enjoyed Mrs. Marvin's company, although he saw her only rarely. Her request for a formal appointment took him by surprise, since she knew she was welcome to drop in on the president at any time. When she arrived in his office, the two made small talk. Mrs. Marvin, a lively woman with special interests in the theater and in music education, was a knowledgeable and seasoned observer of the GW scene. Mrs. Marvin proceeded to pull a dog-eared copy of a brochure listing the various gift opportunities at The George Washington University out of her purse.

"Now, Dr. Elliott, if I understand this correctly, $1 million will name the student center," said Mrs. Marvin.

"Yes, Mrs. Marvin, that is correct," Elliott replied.

Mrs. Marvin then inquired if anyone had yet donated the half million dollars it would take to name the theater on the main floor of the center. Elliott assured her that no one had made such a gift. Without blinking an eye, Mrs. Marvin said, "I would like to take both of the gifts." She would name the student center for her husband and name the theater in memory of her mother and her mother's sisters.

Although President Elliott appreciated Mrs. Marvin's generosity, he doubted she had the money to donate $1.5 million to The George Washington University. He made discrete inquiries of a University accountant who helped Mrs. Marvin with her taxes. Respecting Mrs. Marvin's privacy, the accountant was non-committal. Within a few days, Mrs. Marvin dispelled all of Elliott's doubts by making another appointment to see him. In the University board room at the top of Rice Hall, Lloyd Elliott watched Dorothy Marvin sign over $1,445,000 worth of stock certificates to the University. She

Marvin Center opening,
February 3, 1970.

The Boston Boys and
General Gage, 1775
Henry Bacon, 1875
oil on canvas, 51" x 95"
The George Washington
University Permanent Collection,
Dimock Gallery

GW's Permanent Collection
includes paintings, sculpture,
prints, photographs, and the
decorative arts spanning some
500 years.

(Right) Students from the music department form a wind quintet for the opening of an exhibit in the Dimock Gallery, the University's art gallery. The gallery, which opened in 1966-67, is in the lower level of Lisner Auditorium.

(Below) The Dimock Gallery, holds eight to 10 exhibitions each year, featuring work by GW students, faculty, and alumni artists. Area artists are also invited to participate in thematic shows.

covered the rest of her commitment from other sources. It turned out she had inherited $100,000 in the 1940s and carefully researched the investment possibilities. She decided to buy stock in a Rochester, New York, company. Her handsome profit from Xerox redounded to The George Washington University's advantage.

In this manner, the student center, with its many modern facilities, became the Cloyd Heck Marvin Center, and the stage in the center became the Dorothy Betts Marvin Theatre. The dedication of these facilities took place in February 1971.

In keeping with the confrontational spirit of the times, the event was not without incident. It occurred in the Lisner Auditorium. Friends of the Marvin family and important members of The George Washington University family sat on the ground floor. Students occupied the balcony.

Lloyd Elliott gave a speech in which he lauded the accomplishments of President Marvin. After he spoke, and the applause began, many of the students on the upper level rose and began walking out of the auditorium with clenched fists raised in the air. "It's the Kent State Center, and you know it," one student shouted. The dignitaries seated on the ground level stopped applauding and craned their necks to see what was happening behind them. Elliott assured them that Mrs. Marvin did not mind the disruption. "I'm used to that," she said. "I was the wife of a University president for 32 years." In her remarks, she noted that, "It just goes to show you that they live in one world while we live in another. They have no conception of the world we live in."

In time, the incidents that attended the dedication of the Marvin Center were forgotten and the existence of the center became woven into the very fabric of University life. The fact that the University finally had adequate dining, extracurricular, and social facilities far outweighed the short-term memory of the student disruption.

Over the years, activities in the Marvin Center faithfully reflected the style and tone of student life. At first, for example, the center contained a barbershop, a traditional fixture in a student union. In 1972 the barbershop closed. Robert Dean, who ran Dean's barbershop, lamented "the long hair thing. Kids only get a haircut once every six months...when they have to go home."

Creation of the Marvin Center constituted an impressive achievement on Lloyd Elliott's part, and it was just one of many. Even before the Marvin Center initiated operations, the University opened a large new classroom and office building on G Street. It ultimately took the name of Norma Lee and Morton I. Funger Hall and, with its 172,000 square feet of space, served for many years as the nerve center of the University's academic programs in education and in the social sciences.

MAYDAY

The year in which the Marvin Center was dedicated proved to be the last in which major student disruptions occurred. The 1971 rites of spring at GW featured the Mayday riots. The scenario was by now familiar. GW students attended a rally near the White House. On their way back to the campus, they encountered a group of construction workers at the site of the World Bank Building. When the demonstrators blocked traffic on 20th Street, these workers, peering down from the steel framework of the unfinished building, urged drivers to "run 'em over." Students tried to find common cause with the construction workers, chanting "higher wages for everyone." The workers were not mollified. They already enjoyed high wages and could not comprehend the students' dissatisfaction with the course of American life.

The students did not have time to linger, since the police were hard on their heels. In time, the police cordoned off the campus and arrested anyone who could not produce a GW ID. President Elliott was determined that the University not close this time. The University administration decided to restrict admission to the Marvin Center and the residence halls to GW personnel. "Every effort will be made by the University to see that the regular academic program continues in the days ahead," Elliott said. Unlike the outcome in 1970, it did.

Chicago Tribu

THE WORLD'S GREATEST NEWSPAPER

Friday, August 9, 1974

128th Year—No. 221 © © 1974 Chicago Tribune

Nixon re

'Americ
full-tim

By Frank Starr
and Aldo Beckman
Chicago Tribune Press Service

WASHINGTON, A u g. 8—President
Nixon tonight announced his decision to
resign as the 37th President of the
United States to avoid impeachment for
his role in the Watergate scandal.

The unprecedented but orderly transfer of power to Vice President Ford
will occur at noon tomorrow, with no
interruption of government operation
expected.

Nixon's resignation, the first ever by
an American President, came 21
months after he had won a second
term by one of the largest margins in
history.

BUT IT ALSO climaxed a scandal
that grew out of that election and was
still developing Monday, when the
President admitted his own early

Sports **Final**
★★★★

60 Pages   4 Sections   15¢

e

igns

a needs a

President'

Growth
and Change

AFTER THE REVOLUTION

If the GW student uprisings had little or no effect on the University's decision to engage in a determined course of capital expansion, they did have a permanent effect on University life. Changes in the rules governing dating and life in the residence halls constituted one example. Other changes involved the University's calendar. At the end of January 1971, the faculty voted to schedule exams before Christmas. Gone were the days in which students returned after Christmas to take their examinations.

Some faculty members carped at this alteration of traditional practice. Law professor David Robinson put his complaints in humorous terms. He said that the faculty "were not here to relieve student anxieties. A few years ago, we relieved their anxieties about sex by permitting open dormitory hours. Then we tried to relieve their anxieties about classes by allowing unlimited cuts. Now we're going to abolish reading week to relieve their anxieties about studying."

By 1971, it had become apparent that the tone of student life had changed. In the dormitories, the soft and melodic music of James Taylor began to be heard, in contrast to the more amplified and dissonant tones of hard rock groups such as Led Zeppelin. Students returned to their familiar complaints of alienation, a retreat from the purposeful rhetoric of student revolution. They yearned for greater diversity in the student body—over half of 1971's freshmen came from New York, New Jersey, and Pennsylvania—and some even lamented GW's relatively low admissions standards. Most of the people who applied to GW were accepted.

These were concerns to which Lloyd Elliott was eager to respond. He realized the need to develop a larger endowment that would help to fund stronger educational programs. For this reason, beginning in 1971, he endorsed a 15-year plan that acquired the slogan "building for greatness." This plan was linked with the existing master plan for the expansion of the University. The Burns Law Library, the Marvin Center, and a new classroom building fit into the first stage of this plan.

MORE EXPANSION: A NEW LIBRARY

The next crucial step consisted of the completion of a new main library for the campus. According to then-University Librarian Rupert Woodward, the old library in Lisner Hall had long outlived its usefulness. When this library was built in the 1930s, it might have been adequate for GW's needs. Until 1966, it remained a limited, closed stack operation. Students complained about the low level of lighting and the confused arrangement of the books. The sheer lack of space constituted a much more fundamental inadequacy. The old facility lacked sufficient room for the students who wanted to study and for the professors who wanted to do research. It could house only 400,000 volumes, making it equal in size to many community libraries.

President Lloyd Elliott (right) and Chairman of the Board of Trustees Glen A. Wilkinson (left) present Estelle Gelman with a china bowl at the opening of the Melvin Gelman Library. Mrs. Gelman provided a gift to fund the new library in honor of her late husband's memory.

Completed in 1973, what became the Melvin Gelman Library was, by way of contrast, glorious. It had space for 900,000 volumes and enough room for students to browse in the stacks, not to mention 150 closed studies for faculty and graduate student research and 24 group studies. The basement of the library housed an impressive audio listening facility. The opening of the new library, located at 2130 H Street, helped to shift the campus's center of gravity away from G Street.

The year 1973 also marked the completion of Walter G. Ross Hall, which contained many of the offices, classrooms, and laboratories used for instruction in the medical school, and the adjoining Himmelfarb Health Sciences Library. Before this date many of the medical school functions took place on H Street, between 13th and 14th Streets. Sixty-one years after the establishment of the Foggy Bottom campus, GW had finally managed to put most of its schools into one location and to expand its campus west from 20th Street to beyond 23rd Street.

STILL MORE CONSTRUCTION:
THE SMITH CENTER

In 1975, a final piece of the University's basic structure went into operation in the form of the Charles E. Smith Center for Physical Education and Athletics at 600 22nd Street. In February of that year, the basketball team played its final game at Fort Myer. Beginning in the 1975-1976 season, GW basketball fans no longer needed to cross the river to see their team perform. Instead, the team competed in the Smith Center. As one fan put it, the new center, opened in November 1975, would help bring more of a college atmosphere to GW. As with the other new facilities, the Smith Center both expanded the boundaries of the University and consolidated what were previously widely scattered operations.

In this regard, the fate of the wrestling team was typical. For years, the team practiced in the dungeon-like setting of the GW science hall. With the opening of the Smith Center, it acquired a fully-equipped wrestling gymnasium. Just as with the library, the improvements wrought by the Smith Center were nothing short of remarkable. The center contained a main arena, an auxiliary arena, an eight-lane pool, a wrestling room, seven handball courts, a baseball batting cage, offices for the physical education department, and two saunas. At last, GW had realized Lloyd Elliott's wish that GW students have a place that would allow them to get off the street corners and into a wholesome atmosphere of physical recreation.

Not all of the GW master plan involved the creation of new campus buildings. As part of the plan, the University also built office buildings designed to be rented to others. Such buildings included the World Bank Building, which came to occupy the square block bounded by F, G, 19th, and 20th Streets, the Thomas Edison Building on Pennsylvania Avenue, and the Joseph Henry Building

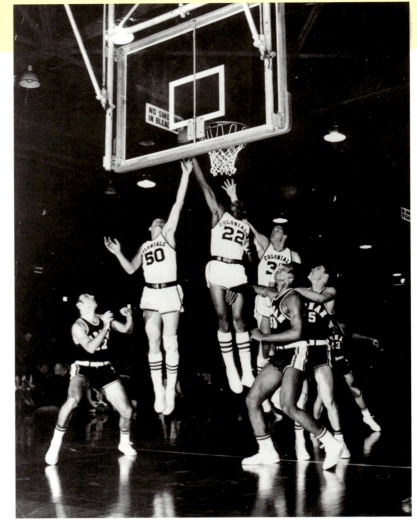

(Above) Before the Smith Center was built, the men's basketball team played their home games at Fort Myer, across the Potomac in Virginia.

(Right) When the Charles E. Smith Center opened in November 1975, the Colonials basketball teams found a permanent on-campus court to host home games.

on Pennsylvania Avenue. The revenue derived from these buildings, in the form of rents paid by such major lessees as the Potomac Electric Power Company and the National Academy of Sciences, helped to finance the Marvin and Smith Centers and other large campus facilities.

THE AESTHETICS OF GROWTH

The superimposition of a new campus on the old one, built largely in the 1930s and 1940s, occasioned its share of controversy. Wolf Van Eckhardt, *The Washington Post* architectural critic, spoke on campus in 1972 and objected to a plan that privileged the new and tore down anything that was old.

Criticism of the University's expansion took two main forms. One line of thought held that the University should not destroy Foggy Bottom by demolishing the townhouses that gave the neighborhood its character. Some in the GW community thought, for example, that the University should develop a tree-shaded, townhoused

Crew began as a club sport at GW in 1958, and as a team sport in the 1960s. Early morning commuters into the District of Columbia can often catch the team practicing on the misty Potomac.

urban campus that blended into the existing landscape. Each time the University demolished an old townhouse, it risked incurring bad publicity from the *Post* and from the neighborhood association. In the summer of 1972, for example, the University removed two townhouses that had stood for more than 50 years at 2027 and 2029 H Street. For some, the short-term reward of more parking spaces did not match the long-term loss of neighborhood identity.

Another line of thought criticized the University not so much for the scale of the buildings it erected as for the lack of imagination in designing them. The Joseph Henry, World Bank, and Thomas Edison buildings strongly resembled each other in their block-like cement structures. Nor would the new library, the Smith Center, the new classroom building, or the Marvin Center win awards for architectural creativity. In many respects these new buildings amounted to 1970's versions of the utilitarian architectural style that had characterized the design of Lisner, Bell, and Stuart Halls in the 1930s. Paradoxically, criticism of GW architecture coincided with the founding of one of the nation's pioneer programs in urban planning and in historical preservation, under the able direction of Dorn McGrath.

AFTERMATH OF THE 1960S

On the surface, GW appeared to be a far more placid place at the end of 1972 than it had been in the four previous years. The Trustee Committee on Students Affairs reported in May 1972 that the academic year just concluding "has been relatively peaceful on the George Washington campus" and credited the changes in the Nixon administration's Vietnam policy for the transformation. The defeat of George McGovern, who was the choice of 65 percent of the students polled on campus, failed to occasion the sort of riot that had occurred in 1968.

President Elliott began 1973 by remarking that the University was in its best shape in years. In September 1973, *The Hatchet* proclaimed that the "days of GW being the 'Holiday Inn of the Revolution' are gone forever." Trustee John Duncan noted in 1974, "Students today are enjoying their work within the system...they realize that less is ultimately accomplished through demonstrations and certain other activist actions."

To be sure, these students differed from their earlier counterparts. In 1975, *The Hatchet* ran a piece that described the drug scene at GW. The article occasioned little outrage or comment. It simply reported that the drug of choice on campus was cocaine, which cost $60 to $90 per gram. Marijuana, widely available on campus, ran about $15 an ounce. The newspaper made no effort to determine what percentage of GW students used these substances.

In fact, however, student activism produced far more than a casual drug scene; nor was it, as the trustees implied, a passing phase in the University's development with no permanent effects. Such a view missed the profound institutional changes that began in the late 1960s and blossomed in the 1970s. One such change involved GW's outreach into the community, as in the legal clinic on 19th Street that the law school helped to start.

In effect, the Urban Law Institute operated as a large public interest law firm, staffed by 30 law students. Although the law school surrendered its association with this institute after only a few years, it nonetheless helped to launch an important outpost of the war on poverty in D.C. The experiment underscored one of the real advantages of a GW education. In 1975, Lloyd Elliott noted that, although GW was not yet in the Ivy League, it encouraged its students "to pursue a kind of parallel education in the city of Washington."

Another, more subtle, form of outreach took the form of the Educational Opportunity Program, which began formal operations in 1969. This program marked a response to a suggestion from the Black Students Union that GW make a stronger commitment to the African-American residents of the D.C. community. In the fall of 1968, GW offered a tuition remission plan to 25 D.C. public high school graduates. In 1969, with the beginning of the Educational Opportunity Program, the number of tuition waivers expanded to 40, and the University put a more complete set of support services in place.

The program involved special recruitment efforts and a free enrichment course that students took in the summer before they entered their freshman year. In this course, the students received intensive instruction in mathematics, including algebra and trigonometry, and in the development of college-level reading skills. During their first semester at GW, the students took no more than four courses, and they had access to free tutoring services throughout their college years.

This program, combined with other efforts to attract black students to GW, helped to bring a welcome diversity to the GW student body. Still, like many experiments, the Educational Opportunity Program (EOP) was not an unqualified success. Only about 60 percent of the students in the program, many of whom continued to live at home, graduated from GW. Often the black students at GW felt isolated, particularly at the beginning of the program when GW enrolled only about 80 in a student body of 13,000. Within several years, however, EOP students were graduating at rates higher than those of the undergraduate student body as a whole.

For those who persevered, the program brought many rewards. The case of Gloria Hollingsworth, who graduated in 1979, was not atypical. She confessed that it was the Educational Opportunity Program, not the University itself, that attracted her to GW. She praised the eight-week summer orientation program, the financial aid that she received, and the "friendly courtesy" of the program directors. When Alba Thomas, then the director of the program, observed that, "Our students are meeting challenges that confront them and are contributing greatly to the University community," she stated the opinion of many.

Today, in its 25th year, the Educational Opportunity Program has more than 200 minority students spread across the undergraduate programs of the University, their presence is a reminder of Lloyd Elliott's steadfast commitment to serving the Washington community.

DIVISION OF EXPERIMENTAL PROGRAMS

Another example of the permanent change that stemmed from the events of the late 1960s involved the Division of Experimental Programs. Through this division, formed in 1969 with the encouragement of Lloyd Elliott, the University responded to demands for curricular reform and for education that grappled with the contemporary problems of Washington. Elliott believed that "experimentation with the undergraduate program is something that ought to be a continuing activity at most campuses." The experiments in general education undertaken at Michigan State and Minnesota were of particular interest to him. Hence, he created the Division of Experimental Programs and put it under the direct charge of the vice president for academic affairs, thus bypassing the deans of the various schools. In effect, the division had the responsibility of reaching across these schools for the purpose of "ongoing, coordinated, University-wide academic development."

Clarence Mondale, universally known as "Pete," became the first director of the division. Elliott later remarked that Mondale, a professor of American studies and the brother of the Minnesota senator, "had all the credentials of an innovator, a creative thinker, one who's willing to take chances and build some new concepts." Mondale's strengths were complemented by Rod French, the associate director and after 1978, director.

The Division of Experimental Programs became a catalyst for innovation in a faculty that tended, among a majority of its members, to have a very conservative educational philosophy. Elliott candidly confessed that it was a way to "pry open and pry into some things in Columbian College that we didn't have a way into otherwise." In a university so preoccupied with physical expansion, the division helped also to expand academic endeavors. Through the division, GW launched programs in such areas as local studies, environmental studies, history and public policy, business ethics, folklore, biomedical ethics, and film studies.

More often than not, these new programs were interdisciplinary endeavors, and often, too, they represented conscious attempts to bridge the cultures of two different schools. As an example, biomedical ethics, which joined the religion, philosophy, and medical school departments in a common endeavor, laid the foundation for

Clarence "Pete" Mondale (left), a GW professor of American studies and the brother of Walter Mondale (right), "had all the credentials of an innovator, a creative thinker, one who's willing to take chances and build some new concepts."

work in the medical humanities that took place in the medical school. Scholarship that explored the relationships between the humanities and the professions and between the humanities and the sciences was a particular interest of Rod French's, one that the division helped to further.

Another important element of the division's work involved what might be described as experiential learning. Through the division, hundreds of GW students participated in internships that allowed them to experience the problems of urban poverty first hand. They went to social service agencies and settlement houses and joined with community activists in a hard-headed look at social conditions. This sort of learning made GW become what one University official termed "more of a legitimate community citizen."

The division chose to operate on the margins of the University's curriculum. However, once one of its endeavors proved successful, the division helped to incorporate it as a permanent part of the University's curriculum. In 1974, for example, the division gave the philosophy department funds to develop an interdisciplinary master's program in philosophy and social policy. In this way, the division helped to focus the department's energies on how the historical and analytical skills of the discipline might be brought to bear upon contemporary problems. The philosophy faculty developed six new graduate seminars. Launched through the division's financial aid, special interest, and encouragement, the master's program in philosophy and social policy became a permanent offering, administered through the Graduate School of Arts and Sciences.

In a similar manner, teachers first recruited by the division on an experimental basis often became regular members of the faculty. Among these were William Becker, a distinguished professor of business history, and John Vlach, an anthropologist and folklorist of international repute.

The Division of Experimental Programs attracted significant outside funding. Through the strong efforts of Trustee Joseph Hughes, the University received $1 million in 1969 for the division from the Richard King Mellon Trusts. Along with the University of Southern California and the Massachusetts Institute of Technology, which also received grants, GW was encouraged to find a means of engaging the problems of the local community. Through the Center for Washington Area Studies, a special course on the history of Washington, a special monograph series on Washington topics, research grants for faculty who worked on Washington-related topics, an award for the best dissertation on Washington, D.C., direct social action projects, and many other means, the Division of Experimental Programs responded to that mandate.

Before the division ended in 1984, with the elevation of Rod French to the office of vice president for academic affairs, it had gone far toward institutionalizing some of the best aspects of the educational reforms of the 1960s. In this way, it also contributed to what Vice President French called the "adaptive survival of the establishment."

SERVING WASHINGTON'S PROFESSIONAL COMMUNITY

The endeavors funded by the division tended to be high-minded, intellectual projects. At the same time, the University continued to develop more pragmatic, and less academic, programs that served the specific needs of the Washington community. These efforts stretched far back into GW's history. In 1940, GW started the Division of Extension, primarily to serve high school teachers in the area. By 1950, this division had blossomed into the College of General Studies.

Within the College of General Studies, a Continuing Education for Women (CEW) program, started in 1964, provided career counseling for women. This program focused on helping homemakers, half of whom already had bachelor's degrees, reenter the labor force. The emphasis tended to be on psychological counseling. Ruth Osborn, M.A.E. '46, Ed.D. '63, guided the program until her retirement in 1979. By this time, the program had already broadened to allow women to gain exposure to influential leaders and politicians in Washington and to permit them to receive very practical job-seeking skills, such as how to write a resume and how to perform well during interviews.

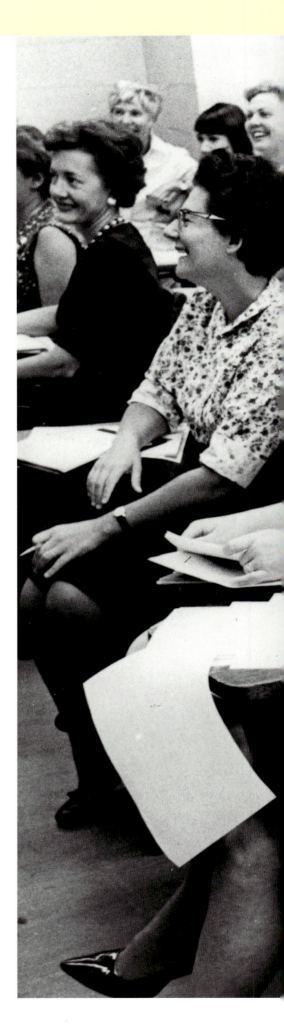

CEW's New Horizons for Women classes, 1965.

*In November 1993, President Bill
Clinton appointed Diane Frankel,
M.A.T. '76, a graduate of the
Museum Education Program,
director of the Federal Institute of
Museum Services. Frankel is
shown here being congratulated by
U.S. Secretary of Education
Richard Riley.*

The Continuing Education for Women team in the 1970s: (left to right) Lisa Judd (office manager); Ruth Osborn (the program's founder); Abbie O. Smith (assistant director of CEW); and Robert Holland (dean of the College of General Studies).

Then a CEW staffer read an article about the Philadelphia Paralegal Institute in Philadelphia, and Abbie Smith, at that time the assistant director of CEW, decided that such a training effort would be good for GW. Attempting to gauge the nature and strength of the demand for paralegals, she set up meetings with lawyers and law school professors. Then, in the fall of 1972, the first class of 28 women and two men came to GW and participated in the first comprehensive University-based certificate program on the East Coast that provided college graduates with formal training as legal assistants. Before these students had finished the American Bar Association-approved program, all of them had been hired—an almost textbook case of effective continuing education.

Encouraged by this success, CEW launched several new programs each year. Entities included the publication specialist program, the landscape design program, the fundraising administrator program, the management specialist program, the information systems specialist program, the Washington representative program, the public relations professional program, and the desktop publishing specialist program. Although the programs were originally designed to aid women in transition, they attracted a significant number of men, perhaps a quarter of the enrollees. CEW became the Center for Continuing Education in Washington in 1981; today it flourishes as the Center for Career Education.

SERVING WASHINGTON'S MUSEUMS
Certificate programs were not the only way in which the University took advantage of its location. Marcella Brenner, who received her GW Ed.D. in 1962 and served on the education school faculty from 1965 to 1982, began her career as a public school teacher and principal. When her students went on field trips to the many museums and other attractions of Washington, she noticed that no effort was made to link their museum experience with the rest of their education. Museums, she realized, were not reaching out to the students, and teachers did not know that there were people in the museums to whom they might turn for help with their lesson plans.

In 1972, Professor Brenner set out to improve this situation. She devised a University-based training program for museum professionals that would bridge the gap between educators in museums and school teachers and that would enhance the educational nature of visits to the museum. She received strong support from Lloyd Elliott and the financial backing of the University and the National Endowment for the Arts.

After a year of planning, the Museum Education Program welcomed its first class in June 1974. It consisted of 24 graduate students who ranged in age from 22 to 47 and who came from many different undergraduate backgrounds. The intensive, one-year interdisciplinary program, which Marcella Brenner directed until her retirement in 1983, took as its basic premises that each student must know one discipline well, must understand the museum as an educational setting, and must be able to interpret museum collections to many different audiences. To gain a sense of how museums and school systems functioned, students supplemented their course work with a field assignment in a school system or museum.

Among those who benefited from this program was Diane Frankel of the class of 1976. In November 1993, when President Bill Clinton appointed her as director of the Federal Institute of Museum Services, an independent agency with a budget of $29 million, she reached the top of her field. Of her GW experience, she recalled that the "courses were very good and the fact that you also went out to Washington's museum resources and had access to most of the professionals, from the directors on down, was wonderful." Of her new position she said, "It's exciting when you're able to elevate colleagues' concerns to the level of national dialogue."

To begin that dialogue, four members of Frankel's GW class attended her swearing-in ceremony. Each of them, including Kathryn Igoe, director of Accreditation and Museum Standards for the American Association of Museums, held important positions in the museum world. By that time, 375 students, including six Fulbright Scholars, had been through the program, and a great many of these students held responsible jobs in the field of museum education.

Although the Museum Education Program was a conspicuous success, GW did not neglect other aspects of museum studies. A master's program in museum studies produced the director of the Dayton Art Institute and the deputy director of the National Museum of American History. Other relevant master's programs included the Master of Arts in the field of American civilization with a concentration on material culture, headed by the same John Vlach who had been recruited by the Division of Experimental Programs. In addition, the University offered the Master of Arts in the field of anthropology with a concentration in museum training, and the Master of Arts in the field of art history with a concentration in museum training. Here was a field that GW had covered, and one in which the curricular reforms of the late 1960s and the work of the Division of Experimental Programs paid substantial dividends.

ISSUES OF THE 1970S

As the 1970s progressed, the challenges to the establishment no longer came from the students. Instead, they stemmed from changing demographics, such as the waning of the baby boomers' college years, and from the country's declining economic fortunes. In January 1974, the Board of Trustees learned, in a scene that was played out at many other colleges, of the existence of a budget crunch. Rises in social security and unemployment compensation taxes, combined with increased costs of fuel oil and declines in enrollment, created an operating deficit. The University responded by "squeezing out" vacant positions and trying to hold down salary increases, not an easy task in the inflationary conditions that prevailed.

GW faced the financial challenges of the 1970s in much better shape than many other American universities, in part because it held so much of its endowment in the form of real estate. In 1977, the University contemplated the last stages of phase one of its master plan, including the construction of what was known as the academic cluster building (and became the Academic Center) on the corner of 22nd and H Streets. The University also considered moving into the second phase of the plan, which called for the construction of a large "income producing center" on the 2000 block of Eye Street. The final phase of the plan, not yet in clear focus, involved the renovation of the older buildings along F and G Streets and the creation of new classrooms and office space.

Despite the University's relative financial strength, it still confronted the demographic challenges of the decade and needed to accommodate an apparent change of interest among prospective undergraduates. In 1976, it became apparent that the kinds of students enrolling at GW were changing. The School of Engineering and Applied Science, the School of Government and Business Administration, and the Graduate School of Arts and Sciences all experienced sharp enrollment increases. At the same time, the University noted a marked decline in Columbian College, particularly in the freshman class. "It's quite clear that there is very little hope that we are going to get large increases in undergraduate students for the next few years," Vice President Harold Bright told the Board of Trustees. He suggested that GW might consider recruiting more foreign students.

(Above) Marcella Brenner, Ed.D. '62, served on the education school faculty from 1965 to 1982. In 1972, she created the Museum Education Program.

(Right) In June 1974, President Elliott presented the Shah of Iran with an honorary degree in Tehran, as their wives looked on. GW has long welcomed students from Iran; the first Iranian students came to the University in 1916.

THE IRANIAN CONNECTION

As it happened, the recruitment of foreign students was a special concern of Lloyd Elliott's, part of his interest in the "internationalization" of GW. One project in which Elliott became involved concerned the forging of links between GW and the government of Iran. In May of 1974, Elliott announced his intention to travel to Tehran to award an honorary degree to the Shah of Iran. When he arrived in that city in June, he praised the Shah for bringing Iran "to the ranks of the foremost nations of our time." Elliott also cited the long relationship between GW and Iran. The first Iranian students came to GW in 1916. The Shah's personal interest in GW began in 1949 when he attended a GW-Georgetown football game.

Elliott hoped that his visit to Iran would bring tangible benefits to the University. GW expected to receive 54 Iranian students, who would study in the School of Engineering and Applied Science. In the School of Government and Business Administration, GW envisioned developing a program for the study of international business. According to the Iranian ambassador, the Shah, who took a personal interest in this program, would provide substantial support for it.

"GWU Welcomes Metro!" read the signs at the July 1977 Foggy Bottom/GWU Metro station opening. The University celebrated the occasion with appearances by President Elliott and by "George" and "Martha Washington." A Metro stop on campus meant that members of the GW community could now avoid the often-clogged bridges over the Potomac River.

Things turned out rather less well than Elliott had hoped. The outbreak of the Iranian revolution ended any chance of a smooth interchange with the government of Iran. The 600 Iranian students at GW in 1979 worried about whether they would ever be able to go home and feared for the safety of their families. Many dropped their courses and paid only the minimum fee that allowed them to remain registered. In November of 1979, with the outbreak of the hostage crisis, relations between GW's Iranian students and the rest of the GW community became strained. According to the student newspaper, the situation approached "an emotional peak not seen here since the late 1960s."

Inevitably, then, the presence of so many foreign students meant that many of the tensions in international relations would be reflected on GW's campus. Still, the fact that GW's student body was so international in its composition greatly enriched campus life. Over the course of the 1970s, the University experienced steadily increasing enrollments of students from foreign countries, with Iran, India, Taiwan, and Nigeria as major sources of students. A great many of these students came to GW to gain technical skills at the School of Engineering and Applied Science.

By 1977, the University had grown closer not only to the international community but also to the rest of the D.C. metropolitan area. In July 1977, the Metro arrived. The University celebrated the occasion with appearances by President Elliott and by "George" and "Martha Washington" at the Foggy Bottom/GWU station on

(Left) Red Lion Row—the row of buildings on Eye Street between 20th and 21st Streets—was in need of much repair in 1980.

(Right) GW renovated these buildings into the popular mixed-use center it is today.

the Blue Line. The opening of the Blue Line meant that members of the GW community could avoid the often-clogged bridges over the Potomac River. National Airport was only a few stops away.

STUDENT PARTICIPATION

If, toward the end of the decade, student activism had waned, the issue of student participation on the Board of Trustees still animated the campus. In 1978, the trustees engaged in what proved to be a prolonged debate with student leaders over granting them the right to elect voting members to the board.

Student government had come full circle at GW. In February 1970, the Student Assembly, in an act meant to emphasize its irrelevance, abolished itself. Once the domain of the fraternities and sororities, who used it to plan campus-wide social events, the student government no longer appeared to have a legitimate place on the GW campus. But by 1975, the students had decided that they wanted their government back and sought, by holding a constitutional convention, to reinvent it.

By the fall of 1976, student government was back in operation, and by 1978, the president of the Student Association sat in on regular Board of Trustees meetings as a guest of the chairman. In addition, one student served as a voting member of the trustees' Committee on Student Affairs and another as a voting member of the Committee on Academic Affairs.

In December 1978, Mark Weinberg, head of the Student Association, argued that the board should go further and put students on the board itself. He told the trustees that they needed input from the "most important group of the University." Another student argued

that there was a lack of interest among GW students because they felt they had no stake in "anything going on." Richard Lazarnick, another of the students who appeared before the trustees, said that students often criticized GW as a "real estate institution that offers courses." It lacked a sense of involvement among the students, he said. Each of these shortcomings could be remedied through student participation on the board.

For the moment, the students failed to sway the trustees, who offered only that there be a student representative on the Committee on University Development. Trustee Tad Lindner argued that every time the University wanted to provide services, it faced "an almost adversary market. I feel we must maintain absolute confidentiality when we are engaged in matters of that nature. I don't have the confidence that could be sustained if we had students on this board." This argument carried the day.

RED LION ROW

As the board debated student participation, the University moved to consolidate its hold over the 2000 block of Eye Street. By 1979, GW had spent more than $2.3 million to purchase most of the buildings along what was known as Red Lion Row. The University hoped to retain some of the commercial character of the row, even as it developed rental office space. Students wanted inexpensive places to eat and small shops to buy necessary sundries, and the University hoped that the new complex, intended to increase the value of the University's endowment, would include a small mall.

Despite this general agreement, the project involved all of the controversies that had attended previous GW building projects. Owners of small businesses such as Dave's 24-Hour Martinizing

and Coleman's restaurant objected to being displaced. The Joint Commission on Landmarks of the National Capital hoped that the small-scale, ornate nature of the townhouses that fronted Eye Street would be retained. These and other issues lingered at the decade's end.

Although the University did not appear to realize it, GW had turned an important corner during the 1970s. At the beginning of the decade, University administrators worried about the institution's very survival in the face of student protests and financial uncertainties. By the end of the decade, these concerns had faded, in part because of Lloyd Elliott's self-described "stubborn" persistence in pressing for GW's physical expansion.

The accumulation of money was never the final objective of this expansion. Rather, GW's growth in the 1970s was part of a conscious strategy for improving educational quality. At first, improvements took the form of restorations to the physical plant to accommodate a new gym, library, student center, and classroom buildings.

Then, with the funds produced by the investment in real estate, the University sought to hire distinguished scholars and augment its already strong faculty.

DISTINGUISHED SCHOLARS

On October 18, 1979, President Elliott made the important announcement that Amitai Etzioni would join the faculty as GW's first University Professor. Etzioni's name commanded instant recognition among sociologists and other social scientists. After graduating with a Ph.D. in sociology from Berkeley, he had taught at Columbia, beginning in 1958. Etzioni also served the Brookings Institution and the Carter White House before accepting the GW appointment.

In the course of a distinguished career, Etzioni had published more than 100 scholarly articles and written or edited 15 books, with topics ranging from the space race to the sociology of complex organizations. "Washington is at the center of the world for public affairs," Professor Etzioni said, "and sociology can make a contribution to assure that the decisions made here are socially valid." The appointment helped to further cement the relationship between the concerns of Washington and those of a leading university. It demonstrated that the University had reached a new and higher level of academic endeavor.

ACADEMIC GAINS IN THE 1980S

In the 1980s, GW consolidated its gains. The decade began with the appointment of Marcus Falkner Cunliffe as GW's second University Professor. Cunliffe was an expert in the history of America and of American literature. Not the least of his virtues from GW's point of view was the fact that he had written *George Washington: Man and Monument*, a biography that many considered the best work of its kind. If the appointment of Amitai Etzioni signaled GW's emergence as a major educational institution in the social sciences,

Marcus Cunliffe's appointment did the same for the University's stature in the humanities.

Tall and good looking with great personal charm, Cunliffe possessed a calm manner and a sharp mind that quickly endeared him to the GW community. He wrote with considerable brio and style, and never seemed to take himself too seriously. Once, asked to list his recreations on a Who's Who form, he scribbled "the pursuit of happiness and filling in questionnaires." Before coming to GW, he

Continued on p. 156

GW welcomed its first University Professor, Amitai Etzioni, in 1979. Today, five professors hold this rank—the highest professorial status at the University. They are (left to right) Etzioni, Peter Caws, Seyyed Hossein Nasr, Kenneth Shaffner, and James Rosenau.

The Graduate School of Education and Human Development

FOSTER MOTHER TO GW PROGRAMS

By any other name, and it has had quite a few, GW's school of education can lay claim to having placed more of its programmatic offspring for adoption within the University than any other unit. "Foster mothering" has been its destiny. Whenever foundling programs have washed up on the shores of academe, the school of education has stood ready to nurture them until they could be placed elsewhere. Over the years, the school has seconded its "human services" program to the sociology department, and its "travel and tourism" program to the school of management. Similarly, its once looked-down-upon physical education department now fends respectably for itself as the athletics department; and its ground-breaking dance program, once disdained by Columbian College, now proudly struts the stage as part of the latter's Department of Theatre and Dance. Even a part of its mysteriously named human kinetics program has been farmed out to the medical school.

To admiring outsiders, however, the school is better known for its degree holders who populate so many schoolrooms and principals' offices from Roanoke to Rockville and beyond. And they, in turn, have built the school's well-deserved local reputation for training high-quality teachers and administrators. On the score of quality, long-time faculty may be excused for reminding the forgetful that the school has several times produced an annual crop of Phi Beta Kappa nominees greater than that of any liberal arts department. Nor will they let anyone forget that Lynda Bird Johnson attended their school.

Teachers' College Class of 1911, as shown in this Cherry Tree yearbook photograph.

(Right) Future Teachers of America, 1953. First row (left to right): J. Boswell; J. Inscoe; M. Munson; J. Williams; C. Smith; and T. Jones. Second row (left to right): A. Mitchell; R. Quinlan; L. Vance; E. Baker; J. DiCaprio; I. Sweeney; and L. Burnett. Boswell—still associated with GW—has been teaching at the University since 1958.

(Left) Reading Clinic, the predecessor of the Reading Center.

(Right) Professor Dorothy Moore (in checkered suit) with her class of elementary student teachers.

The year 1960, as well as any other, offers an insight into the school's striking impact on the educational milieu of the Metropolitan region. That year, it enrolled more than 1,100 degree candidates, most of them from the Washington area. The school had 20 full-time faculty, 25 part-time professional specialists, and a program of more than 100 teachers and administrators supervising student teaching in nearby schools.

Both before and after the booming 1960s, however, the picture was quite different. Teacher training and the University's current name, "The George Washington University," both came into being in 1904. "Education," though it languished at first with fewer than a dozen faculty, gradually metamorphosed from a University "division" in 1907, to a "teachers' college" in 1909, to a "school of education" in 1928. By this time, its faculty were fielding departments of education, educational psychology,

and home economics. In 1932, a year before it began its doctoral program, the school shouldered the thankless chore of offering required physical education classes to all undergraduates. Created separately for men and women, these classes persevered, despised by students and patronized by Columbian's professors until the college quietly dropped the physical education requirement during the turbulent '60s.

Whether in the era of G.I. Bill or that of desegregation, the school has always found a distinctive niche. While, like other schools of education after World War II, GW's served a bumper crop of young G.I.s, it also re-tooled a remarkable number of retired military officers, persons already trained in math and science whose degrees from GW gave them

a welcome second career. Spreading out across the metropolitan area, many quickly rose to become principals and superintendents, *in loco parentis* to the generation of baby boomers. And from their elevated positions they also became a ready-made network for placing subsequent generations of GW teacher-trainees.

Equally in service to minorities, with the ink barely dry on the Supreme Court's decision in the case of *Brown v. Board of Education*, GW's school of education led the University in facing up to the opportunities and challenges of desegregation. Its classes were soon crowded not with only with black teacher applicants from the District but also from Virginia where segregationists, fighting some of their early battles against

integration, paid black applicants to apply out of state. As early as 1955, black students predominated in GW's education classes. That some of these individuals came ill-prepared was part of the challenge. Professor John Boswell recalls Dean James Fox pointing at him and saying, "It's your job to make sure they pass." For Boswell this meant tutoring sessions, a task that he and other faculty undertook with a will.

Elsewhere in the 1960s, standards may have crumbled in the face of student activism, but not in the school of education. Perhaps because would-be teachers, like engineering students, had professional goals in view, faculty were able to maintain time-honored curricula. At a time when specifically required liberal arts courses were dropping off the

Columbian College screen, the school of education managed to keep them a central focus for their own freshmen and sophomores. By the late '60s, the school could boast that its undergraduate majors in education took more physics and chemistry courses than any of the liberal arts students, except majors in those departments.

Because maintaining high standards has always been a concern, the school also kept its "junior college." Long after Columbian had abandoned its own A.A. degree, education students who planned to go on for the B.A. had to re-apply at the end of their sophomore year, a break in the process that gave faculty an opportunity to winnow out freshmen and sophomores whose performance gave too little promise.

(Left) A student teacher puts her lessons to work in a real classroom.

(Below) Students attend an elementary school developmental assessment lecture in Funger Hall, Circa 1970s.

A different threat to standards surfaced during the Vietnam War when more than one anti-war protester showed up to register, all too obviously hoping for a draft deferment. They got a chilly reception. Professor Carole St. Cyr quickly built a reputation for spotting applicants who were more intent on avoiding military service than in pursuing careers in teaching.

The '70s, by contrast, saw a turnabout in enrollments that for awhile cast doubt on the school's future. Undergraduate programs withered alarmingly as earlier "pools" of students dried up and rising tuition drove many of them to less costly state-run schools. For the faculty, saving their programs meant learning to specialize. To give its mission sharper purpose, the school's emphasis shifted to graduate education. In the process, it adapted to newly perceived educational needs. In the late '60s, it sought and received government funding for its new special education program, and later reached out to the community by training counselors as well as teachers. Today, the school is down to three lean but flourishing graduate programs: teacher preparation and special education; educational leadership; and a Department of Human Services. Such fine tuning helps explain the school's remarkable renaissance in the past 10 years.

Alumni, who since 1994 have known it as the Graduate School of Education and Human Development, recall classes in adult and child development taught by a kindly, scholarly Martha Rashid; or courses in educational leadership under the school's vastly knowledgeable and gently opinionated John Boswell who, with Michael Castleberry, another old-line southern gentleman, mixed classroom humor with a common sense approach to subject matter; or the thoughtful, quiet reserve of Don Linkowski, scholarly and much-published in the field of counseling.

Recently, Special Education Chair Maxine Freund, who describes herself modestly as a well-funded grantswoman, interviewed Rita Ives, founder of GW's special education program. Ives told how, in company with GW psychologists Gardner Murphy and Beatrice Cornish, and working with counterparts at Georgetown, they won the first interdisciplinary grant from the U.S. Department of Education to study what were then referred to as "handicapped and disabled children." "We beat the nation," Ives said, "in the sense that we were doing early childhood training before there was a federal mandate to identify children who were at risk or disabled." As for the program's influence closer to home, she allowed:

"There is not a school in the metropolitan area—public or private—preschool through high school—that has not been impacted by the philosophy, commitment, and programs of the special education department." From the Education of All Handicapped Children Act in 1975 to the passage of the Americans with Disabilities Act in 1990, GW's education professors, such as Julia Taymans, have led the way.

Always an innovator, John Boswell recalls the time he recruited President Lloyd Elliott to teach a course in University administration. The president's brush with hands-on teaching produced an anecdote, which, to be understood, requires the reader to know the deep suspicion with which the University registrar views after-the-fact changes in a student's grade. Professors are required to explain in writing why they are asking to raise a grade already recorded. Rather than make explana-

(Above) Faculty from the Reading Center take a group of their young students to the Mall for a writing exercise. While Jimmy Carter served as president, his daughter, Amy, attended special classes at the Reading Center.

tions that might suggest soft-heartedness or worse, professors will often plead to having made a mathematical miscalculation in what "should have been" a higher grade.

Toward the close of Elliott's first semester at GW, one of his students had failed to hand in his assignments. Elliott phoned Boswell and asked what he should do. "Flunk him," said Boswell. Long pause, then Elliott replied, "Well, yes, I guess I could do that." John went on: "If the student hands in the work later and it's acceptable, you can raise his grade. Then, like the rest of us, you can lie to the registrar about why you did it."

Anecdote aside, the president's willingness to be recruited to the classroom reflected Lloyd Elliott's strong conviction that University administrators should stay in touch with the institution's central teaching mission. As he later confided to Boswell: "I'd forgotten how time-consuming and exacting teaching is," a truism that resonates with all teachers, but especially with the teachers who teach teachers and whose school marches proudly under the University's banner of excellence.

Continued from p. 150

had taught at the University of Sussex and established himself as perhaps the leading English practitioner of American studies. As *The Washington Post* put it, Cunliffe knew "more about America than most Americans." Cunliffe himself admitted that being in America gave him a sense of energy and that he admired the "good sense" and the "skepticism" of the country. *The Times of London* described him as a "true mid-Atlantic man."

For a decade, until his death in September 1990, Cunliffe added to the stature of the GW history and American studies departments. Humanities professors at other schools invariably associated GW and Marcus Cunliffe. Cunliffe, for his part, stayed aloof from departmental and University politics. Instead, even as he continued to pursue his studies of such topics as the history of property and revised his classic *Literature of the United States*, he remained dedicated to the University, doing more than his share of teaching and aiding the University in job searches and other important matters. Robert Kenny, a GW history professor who served as dean of Columbian College at the end of the 1980s, characterized Cunliffe as a "monumental figure in American and social history who had the respect and admiration of scholars all over the world."

Soon after Cunliffe's appointment came news of a $1.5 million gift from Estelle Gelman, the widow of a Washington businessman who had graduated from GW's School of Government and Business Administration in 1940. The interest on the money would be used to support the library. In recognition of this gift, the library officially became the Melvin Gelman Library on May 14, 1980.

Started on such an optimistic note, 1980 ended with the good news of even more funds available for library acquisitions. On December 17, 1980, the University received notification that it had won an $800,000 challenge grant from the National Endowment for the Humanities (NEH). President Elliott said that the grant, which GW would match on a three-to-one basis, would help to launch the "largest financial campaign in support of academic programs in the history of the University."

Rod French, who headed the team that wrote the NEH grant proposal, said that the bulk of the money, in addition to supporting the library, would be used to endow three chairs in the humanities. These new professors would come from the traditional humanities disciplines, such as philosophy, religion, literature, and history, but, as French put it, "they will only be occupied by people who can relate what they're doing to professional studies."

French and other University administrators knew that the humanities at GW and elsewhere faced relatively hard times. Through the grant, the University hoped to strengthen the humanities and also to forge linkages between them and the thriving programs in business, science policy, educational policy, environmental policy, and energy policy. In this manner, the new professorships reinforced

the work already being done in the Division of Experimental Programs and furthered French's strategy of the adaptive survival of the liberal arts.

The University decided to take its time in appointing the new University Professors in the humanities. Not until January 1982 did President Elliott announce that Professor Peter Caws would join the faculty in September as University Professor of Philosophy. Caws had done his undergraduate work at the University of London in physics and his graduate work at Yale in philosophy. In his academic work, he wrote about the philosophy of science, including *The Philosophy of Science: A Systematic Account* (1965), and about French philosophy, including *Sartre* (1978). Caws had previously taught at Michigan State, the University of Kansas, and Hunter College (where he served as chair of the philosophy department). At the City University of New York Graduate Center, he also directed the Ph.D. program in philosophy.

Like the other University Professors, Caws was a major figure in his field and a great intellectual asset for GW. Outside of the classroom, he was also a tremendously engaging person, with interests in such endeavors as cooking, bicycling, and music.

SEYYED NASR

Seyyed Hossein Nasr, a scholar of Islamic studies, became the fourth University Professor and the second professor hired using money from the NEH challenge grant. Born in Iran, Nasr left in 1945 to study physics and mathematics at The Massachusetts Institute of Technology. Remaining in this country, he took his graduate degrees at Harvard in the history of science, with a special emphasis upon Islamic science and philosophy. He then embarked on a distinguished career as professor of science and philosophy at Tehran University. He enjoyed an international reputation and his many books, such as *Three Muslim Sages, Ideals and Realities of Islam*, and *Science and Civilization in Islam*, appeared in English, French, Italian, Spanish, German, Arabic, Persian, and Japanese. He was the first Muslim ever to give the celebrated Gifford Lectures in the Philosophy of Religion at the University of Edinburgh.

In 1979, the turmoil in Iran made it necessary for him to leave again. He returned to the United States, securing a post as a professor at Temple, before receiving the call from George Washington. Ensconced on the seventh floor of Gelman, Nasr described himself as an old-fashioned scholar who did nearly all of his own research and eschewed the use of a word processor. Like many other writers, he claimed that he did most of the work while doing other things, such as walking around campus. When he sat down to write about Sufism, the mystical dimension of Islam, or about some other aspect of Islamic culture, he found that "the words begin to flow and I write very rapidly." In this manner, he remained a prodigiously productive scholar and an extraordinary asset to GW.

(Left to right) University Professor
Peter Caws, Vice President
Roderick French, Professors Lois
Schwoerer, Phyllis Palmer, and
Sera Morgan attend an exhibit in
the Gelman Library's Special
Collections on the work of
University Professor Marcus
Cunliffe, who died in Sept. 1990.

UNIVERSITY LIFE IN THE '80S

As the scholars sat in their Gelman towers, the ongoing work of
the University continued. Students at the University pursued their
studies, many managing to take full advantage of Washington's
opportunities. In the fall of 1981, construction began on the 2000
Eye Street complex. In 1986, the University released a plan outlin-
ing its hope to purchase all land within the boundaries of
Pennsylvania Avenue, 19th Street, Virginia Avenue, and 24th Street.

When Donald E. Koenig graduated in 1980, he offered a personal
inventory of those opportunities. During his four years at GW, he
had met Hubert Humphrey only four weeks before he died;
watched Jimmy Carter walk down Pennsylvania Avenue on
Inauguration Day; dined at the Georgetown home of one of his
state's senators; watched Pope John Paul II give a speech on the
front lawn of the White House; seen the treasures of King

Tutankhamen at the National Gallery; celebrated the 100th anniversary of *The Washington Post* at a party given by Katharine Graham for employees; endured tear gas from Park Police while observing pro- and anti-Shah forces battle on the Ellipse; observed Sadat and Begin sign a peace treaty; and protested at the Iranian Embassy with 200 other Washington-area residents. Such an extraordinary portfolio of personal experiences could only be acquired at The George Washington University.

RONALD REAGAN CONVALESCES

In 1981, Ronald Reagan, a new neighbor along Pennsylvania Avenue, moved into the White House. On March 30, employees of The George Washington University Medical Center made his personal acquaintance under trying circumstances. Shot by a gunman who reportedly hoped to win the affection of actress Jodie Foster, Reagan entered the GW emergency room and told his wife, "Honey, I forgot to duck." About to go under the surgeon's knife to remove the 22-caliber bullet that had lodged in his left lung, he joked about whether or not the surgeon was a Republican. "We're all Republicans today," was the reply. During his recovery, Reagan said, "God must have been sitting on my shoulder." Dr. Dennis O'Leary, GW's dean for clinical affairs, became something of a media star as he issued concise but informative bulletins on the president's improving condition.

Ronald Reagan's hospitalization brought national attention to GW and helped to highlight the University's many positive features. Perhaps as a result, applications for the freshman class increased during the next admissions cycle. In May of 1982, Elliott told the trustees that the class entering the next year would be the strongest academically since 1970. Those who chose GW knew that they would receive a front-row seat to observe the Reagan revolution or the many other events that took place in Washington. In September 1983, for example, any GW student who cared to could walk over to the Marvin Center and watch former Senator George McGovern launch his bid for the 1984 Democratic nomination for president.

DEPARTURES

In the spring of 1983, the University reached the end of an era with the announced retirements of Calvin Linton, dean of Columbian College, and Harold Bright, provost and vice president for academic affairs. That year also marked the retirement of Seymour Alpert, vice president for development. The careers of each of these individuals spanned the Marvin and Elliott eras.

Alpert had been associated with the University for more than 30 years, first serving GW as a faculty member in the medical school. Si Alpert, one of GW's best known officers in the broader Washington community, played a significant role in raising funds first for the medical school and then for the expansion of the entire campus.

Linton had graduated from GW in 1935. He did his graduate work at Johns Hopkins, writing a dissertation about Shakespeare on the modern English stage. After leaving Hopkins, Linton got a job teaching English at Queens College in North Carolina. Like so many of his generation, World War II interrupted his academic career. He served in the Navy, first in the Office of Naval Intelligence and then in minecraft in the Atlantic. When the war ended, Linton returned to GW as a professor of English. In the course of his career, he wrote four books and published 40 articles

on literary theory and criticism. Linton said that of all the things that he did at GW, including serving as dean, he derived the most pleasure from teaching English.

Reflecting on his long career, Linton came to believe that GW did not yet know how good it was. GW's image did not match its performance. "We have not yet got a handle on how to project our excellence," he observed.

Bright came from a different side of the University. He arrived at GW in 1954 to serve as a statistician in the Army's Human Resources Research Office. After a brief stint working at General

Electric, he returned to GW in 1958 to serve as chair of the statistics department. During his GW tenure, he often handled technically demanding projects for the University, such as serving as the first director of the computer center.

ARRIVALS

The departures of Linton and Bright caused Elliott, who was himself reaching retirement age, to contemplate the University's future. In January of 1984, he took two important steps. The first concerned personnel. He decided to divide Bright's job as provost and vice president for academic affairs into two separate jobs. He

While recuperating at the GW Hospital, Ronald Reagan received "Get Well" wishes from government employees posing on the steps of the Old Executive Office Building.

nominated William D. Johnson, known throughout the campus as "Budget" Bill Johnson, as provost. Johnson would concentrate on the financial management of the University. For the post of vice president for academic affairs, he selected Rod French, the head of the Division of Experimental Programs.

Rod French grew up in Oregon and received his undergraduate degree in 1954 from Kenyon College where he graduated summa cum laude and was elected to Phi Beta Kappa. Already interested in the ecumenical movement, he read the works of Paul Tillich and Reinhold Niebuhr in college and decided to pursue graduate studies in theology. After five years of study divided between the Union Theological Seminary in New York and the Episcopal Theological School in Cambridge, he left A.B.D. for a job in Geneva as director of student work for the World Council of Churches. Returning home in 1964 and engaging in freelance writing, he became increasingly interested in the civil rights movement. In 1967, he took a job as special assistant to the director of the office of public affairs at the Peace Corps, before deciding in 1968 to seek an American studies Ph.D. at GW. Working at the outset with Pete Mondale and others, he taught the course on "Contemporary Issues in American Society" and helped administer the Division of Experimental Programs.

When Elliott nominated French for the job of academic vice president, he noted that French had worked with great effectiveness to bridge departments and University divisions and offer new courses and programs. In so doing, French had proved his worth as an administrator and had demonstrated an ability to take a panoramic look at the University. Like any good administrator, he strove to see the University not as a collection of warring fiefdoms, but as something cohesive.

The second step that Elliott took in January 1984 consisted of appointing a University-wide group to consider the University's future direction and needs. This group, chaired by Associate Provost Marianne Phelps and known as the Commission on the Year 2000, drew its membership from the law school, education school, medical center, business and public administration school, the Sino-Soviet Institute, and the religion department. Completing its work in May 1985, the group issued a report on future goals that commanded attention from the president, the Board of Trustees, and other influential segments of the University community.

In the summer of 1985, Lloyd Elliott completed 20 years on the job and said that he felt terrific. He took particular pride in building a stronger faculty and in improving the size and quality of the libraries. He added, "We can become a great university within a relatively short period of time and take our place alongside the best universities in the world."

Rod French quickly took hold as vice president for academic affairs. In one of his first actions, he established GW's University Seminars program as a means for faculty from several departments to discuss scientific, policy-related, or scholarly problems and to draw on the expertise of other authorities in the Washington community.

Over the years, the seminars have provided a forum for some of GW's most prominent scholars. The seminar on Central and Eastern Europe featured the work of Professor Sharon Wolchik, a prominent authority on the politics of that region and a member of GW's nationally recognized political science department. Peter Caws helped to organize the seminar on human sciences, which led to a full-scale graduate program in that field. Peter Budetti, who held a joint appointment in the law and business schools and who possessed considerable expertise in the field, presided, along with several of his colleagues, over the health policy seminar. A group of historians, political scientists, and anthropologists organized a seminar on Andean culture and politics. Another group of classicists established a seminar on ancient Mediterranean cultures. All in all, the University Seminars were another example of the vitality of GW's intellectual life.

*Many distinguished faculty partici-
pated in GW's University
Seminars—designed as a means for
faculty from several departments
to discuss scientific, policy-related,
or scholarly problems:*

*(Far left) Peter Budetti, GW's
Harold and Jane Hirsh Professor
of Health Care Law and Policy, as
well as a professor of law and of
health care sciences, presided over
a health policy seminar.*

*(Left) Sharon Wolchik, professor
of political science and international affairs and a prominent
authority on the politics of Central
and Eastern Europe, spoke at a
seminar on Central and Eastern
Europe.*

NIGHT SCHOOL

Improvement in academic quality did not come without cost. For
years, GW had acquired a reputation as a place where government
employees and others in Washington could come to study at night.
Many graduate programs tried to accommodate the needs of those
who worked full time during the day. The graduate course schedule
relied heavily on classes that began at four in the afternoon. Some
professors offered classes that started at 8 p.m. and did not con-
clude until 10 p.m. At that hour, many graduate students could be
seen wearily walking across campus on their way home.

Some of the programs even featured classes held close to the work-
places of those enrolled in the program. One could study for a master's degree in legislative affairs, for example, on Capitol Hill, and
take engineering courses in Crystal City. Still other programs were
explicitly designed to be offered in the evening.

Of these evening programs, the one in the law school had become
something of a Washington institution. The ranks of assistant secre-
taries of the executive departments, many of whom were permanent civil servants rather than political appointees, contained an
inordinate number of people who had studied law in GW's evening
law school. They studied at night because they were too busy and
too poor to do so during the day. When they rose to prominence,
they remembered their GW experiences with special fondness.

In 1985, the law school decided to phase out the evening law program. Dean Jerome Barron explained that the pool of applicants
for the evening program was shrinking and the pool for the day
program was expanding. The evening program could no longer
admit enough qualified applicants to make it viable. President
Elliott endorsed Dean Barron's recommendation. When Elliott had

arrived in Washington, he had been advised to discontinue the
evening law school by the executive secretary of the Association of
American Law Schools. He investigated the matter and discovered
that three-quarters of the people in the evening program were better qualified than their counterparts in the regular program. Twenty
years later, Elliott realized that the situation had changed: the day
students generally had higher academic qualifications than the
evening students, and the gap was widening. Many people applied
to the night school only as a means of eventually transferring to the
day school. The hard fact was that, if the law school hoped to
become one of the top 10 law schools in the country, it needed to
drop the evening program.

Not all of the trustees agreed with Elliott and Barron. Joseph
Wright, a board member, was himself a graduate of the evening law
school. Discontinuing it presented him with what he described as
an "emotional problem." Wright said that he would not have had a
chance to attend law school if it were not for the GW program. The
University should not discontinue a program that offered
Washingtonians a chance to combine work and study.

In the end, the board agreed on a compromise measure that phased
out the evening law school program, but continued to offer a full
range of evening courses. The incident symbolized a cultural clash
between the old GW, always a faithful servant of the working
Washington community, and the new GW, forever mindful of GW's
increasing prominence as a major research university. In moving
from the old to the new, the University faced the continuing question of what to preserve and what to discard. The debate over the
fate of the evening law program posed that question in stark terms.

GW students have volunteered their time to help out at Miriam's Kitchen, which fed hundreds of homeless citizens every week.

TOWARD THE YEAR 2000

To be sure, GW's rise within the world of higher education brought considerable rewards. In mid-decade, the University attracted the largest freshman classes in its history. The endowment rose as well. By 1985, it had reached a level of $169.8 million, over half of which took the form of real estate investments. In that year as well, the University, aware that a more sophisticated curriculum required more classroom time, increased the length of the semesters to 14 weeks.

In May 1985, the University turned its attention to the report of the Commission on the Year 2000. Accepting the report, Elliott spoke of the need for the University to "position" itself in the educational marketplace according to its special strengths and its students' special needs. He said that the "academic and financial foundations (were) firmly in place." It was "time to translate our vision of excellence into reality."

The report underscored the fact that GW was a mature institution with a growing endowment (41st among American universities). Between 1970 and 1985, the University had added 2.2 million square feet of new academic facilities and increasing numbers of faculty members were nationally recognized in their fields.

To consolidate these gains and prepare for the future, the commission recommended that the University continue to emphasize research. Research, according to the commission, should be a priority in hiring, tenure, promotion, and salary decisions. The commission also suggested that more attention should be paid to general education in the undergraduate curriculum and called for more instruction in writing. The commission hoped that all GW undergraduates would acquire at least minimal competence in mathematics. Finally, the commission advised that the University make a big push to develop its international programs and its programs in government and public policy. The School for Public and International Affairs should become simply the School for International Affairs. A Center for the Study of Public Policy should aid in developing new multidisciplinary research programs. All in all, it amounted to an ambitious program, but Elliott felt it was within the University's reach.

Among other things, the report provided the springboard for the University's first comprehensive development campaign. Conducted from 1985 to 1990, the Campaign for George Washington exceeded by $10 million its goal of $75 million. Trustee Oliver Carr, Jr., who later chaired the board, served as chairman of the capital campaign.

Continued on p. 171

The School of Business and Public Management

When the School of Business and Public Management acquired its present name in 1990, Dean Benjamin Burdetsky commented, "the business program is 80 percent of what we do." He added that "we teach students how to be more effective managers." In some sense, that mission has remained the same since the school began in 1898 as the Department of Comparative Jurisprudence and Diplomacy. Over time, however, the school has broadened its focus from a near-exclusive concern with government to a broader interest in business and the interactions of the private and public sectors.

THE BEGINNINGS

In common with nearly all of GW's schools, the School of Business and Public Management changed its title frequently between 1898 and 1928. Among the school's predecessors were the Department of Politics and Diplomacy (1905) and the College of Political Sciences (1908). In 1928, a seminal event in the University's history occurred, with the establishment of the School of Government. It offered undergraduate courses in government as well as courses that prepared undergraduates for the foreign service. The foreign service branch of the school ultimately evolved into the Elliott School of International Affairs.

THE MASONIC CONNECTION

The establishment of the School of Government depended in large part on what has been called the Masonic Connection (see the section on the Elliott School, page 109). At some point in the 1920s, the League of Masonic Clubs became interested in having properly trained people enter the foreign service.

(Above) In 1927, the Masons gave GW $1 million for the then-School of Government. The Masonic connection continued at GW in 1954 with the establishment of the Scottish Rite Fellowships and the Wolcott Scholarships.

(Left) The 1940 holders of the National League of Masonic Club Scholarships. Seated (left to right): Franklin P. Hillman, GW President Cloyd Heck Marvin, and Charles K. Hellriegel, Jr. Standing (left to right): John E. Mellor; Edward L. Souweine; Neal S. Hendrickson; and Blake Ehrlich.

(Above) Col. Lyman D. Bothwell,
Dean Arthur E. Burns, Harry W.
Kettles, and Sally Parker attend at
a student conference in the School
of Government, 1955.

(Left) His Excellency Si Haj
Mohammed Mokhtar Temsamani,
counselor for information and cultural relations of the Sherifian government in French Morocco, lectures students in the Hall of
Government on the Moroccan
political situation, Nov. 14, 1955.

In this decade of debate over immigration restriction and of concern that
America might abandon its isolationist
stance in the wake of World War I, the
Masons thought it inappropriate that
only Georgetown University, a Catholic
institution, offered this type of training.

Whatever the Masons' motivation, their
largess proved invaluable to GW. On
December 28, 1927, the Board of
Trustees accepted a gift of $1 million
from the Masons with the understanding that the gift would revert if at any
time GW ceased to be nonsectarian. The
fact that George Washington, Luther
Rice, and President Cloyd Heck Marvin
were all dedicated Masons helped to
cement the deal. With this gift, GW started the School of Government.

In 1954, Sovereign Grand Commander
Luther Andrew Smith and President
Marvin, with the consent and support of
the Grand Council, established the

Scottish Rite Fellowships. These fellowships were granted to qualified students
for one year of graduate study. A second
contribution that year became the financial foundation of the Wolcott
Scholarships, sponsored by the High
Twelve International and named for E.P.
Wolcott. These scholarships were
awarded for graduate study toward a
master's degree in preparation for government service at the federal, state, or
local levels.

The Masonic generosity continued
beyond 1928 to the present era in which
President Stephen Joel Trachtenberg,
himself a Mason, presides over GW.

GETTING DOWN
TO BUSINESS
Until 1952 the school, which had begun
to grant master's degrees in 1931,
offered graduate programs that led only
to the Master of Arts in Government.

Even by then, however, tensions had
begun to develop within the faculty
among those interested in business
administration and those interested in
public administration. When Arthur
Edward Burns took over as dean in
1948, he had recommended that a separate school of business be established.
He wanted the School of Government to
be more closely allied with the Department of Politics and the Department of
Economics.

Although President Marvin and the
trustees failed to follow this advice, they
did allow the school to broaden its
degree offerings in the 1950s to include
a Master of Arts in Public Administration
and a Master of Arts in Business
Administration. The trustees, realizing
that business had become a larger concern to the school than government, put
both business and international affairs
into the school's title in October 1960.

(Above) Gen. Colin Powell spoke at an alumni gathering in 1987. He is shown here with Dean Norma Loeser. Powell, one of GW's famous alumni, graduated from GW with an M.B.A. in 1971.

(Left) Vice President Roderick French, Dean Benjamin Burdetsky, and GW President Stephen Joel Trachtenberg cut the ribbon at the renaming of the school—from the School of Government and Business Administration to the School of Business and Public Management.

(Below) The U.S. Army Old Guard leads the commencement march to the Smith Center, 1985.

As an important entity within the GW academic community, the school had acquired its own building on the corner of 21st and G. Completed in 1938, the Hall of Government was dedicated on the 150th anniversary of the adoption of the United States Constitution. The building, whose cornerstone contains a bible and a University catalogue, owed its existence to the generosity of Hattie M. Strong. In 1980, the formal architectural design of the school changed when the Hall of Government was joined to Monroe Hall by means of a four-story and basement connector.

THE DEFENSE CONNECTION

In the postwar era, the school became heavily involved in programs related to the nation's defense. Beginning in 1951, faculty members from the school organized and presented a non-credit, three-week program called the Air Force Commanders Course, later renamed the

(Above) Col. Frederick Gregory, GW alumnus (M.S.A. '77), far right, has flown several NASA space shuttle missions.

(Right) Attending GW affords students opportunities to work in the federal government—including the White House.

Air Force Resources Management Program. Each year this program brought six groups of 100 Air Force officers and senior civilian employees to the campus for three weeks of study in management. The Air Force Chief of Staff, General Hoyt S. Vandenberg, addressed the opening sessions. Regular faculty participants included Elmer L. Kayser, who later became the University historian. The program ended in 1957 with the graduation of the 38th class.

Not to be outdone, the Navy requested a nine-month course for senior officers. Inaugurated in 1951, this program ultimately became the Navy Graduate Financial Management Program. Beginning in 1954, the school also offered the Air Force Advanced Management Program. This full-year, 50-hour program prepared field-grade officers for advanced management work. Each year's class consisted of 35 to 40 officers.

THE MODERN ERA

In 1966, James Dockeray arrived as dean, and during a tenure that lasted until 1973 he transformed and unified the school. Despite Herculean efforts, however, Dockeray failed to get the school's undergraduate and master's programs in business administration accredited. That task fell to Peter Vaill. When GW President Lloyd Elliott interviewed Vaill, a student of organizational behavior who had studied at the Harvard Business School with the pioneers in that

field, for the job as dean, the talk centered on accreditation. Either get the school accredited or quit trying, Elliott said. Vaill, who had previously taught at Connecticut and the University of California at Los Angeles, got the school accredited.

On Vaill's watch, the quality of the school's offerings continued to improve. He took the job in part because he recognized that GW was a unique place for the study of management. Unlike most business schools, the School of Government and Business Administration also included the study of government, health care, and urban systems in its comprehensive curriculum. In 1965, to cite one example, the school began graduate instruction in urban and regional planning. In 1968, the trustees authorized a separate degree, the Master of Urban and Regional Planning, which flourished until the early 1980s.

In 1964, the school created a department of health care administration. Five years later, the school instituted a new master's degree in health care administration, which eventually became a master's degree in health services administration. By 1973, when Vaill came to GW, he was told that half of the hospital administrators in the area had degrees from GW. Those administrators could lay claim to having studied with some of the leaders of the field who recognized, long before the present health-care crisis, that hospitals were complex organizations that required specialized management skills. Steve Eastaugh literally

wrote the textbook in the field. Peter Budetti, who has a joint appointment in the law school, continues GW's tradition of leadership in the field of health policy.

In 1976, the school decided to take an innovative approach to doctoral education. Instead of following a rigid schedule of required courses, doctoral students at GW had the opportunity to create their own program of study. In that way, students who came from widely diverse backgrounds enjoyed the freedom to do what made educational sense for them. Some requested and received intensive instruction in quantitative techniques; others, who might already have acquired those skills on the job, took courses from GW's excellent faculty in organizational behavior. Still other academically accomplished students proceeded directly to the thesis. The program enjoyed almost instant success. Today, the school turns away the vast majority of the applicants because there simply is not room for them.

In the 1970s, the school benefited from the Iranian connection. When Lloyd Elliott went to Iran in 1974, he took Dean Vaill and Professor Phillip D. Grub, then serving as the special assistant to the president for international affairs. In August of that year, GW received $1 million from the government of Iran to establish the Aryamehr Professorship of International Management. Professor Grub became the first incumbent of that professorship.

In addition to her teaching, Susan Tolchin, professor of public administration, has written a series of well-received books on deregulation and other topics. She, along with fellow faculty members, also works closely with many government organizations in assessing the effectiveness of various programs and agencies.

The Iranian government hoped that GW would go further and help to establish a college of management at Reza Shah the Great University. School officials, led by Norma M. Loeser (who became dean in 1979), among others, prepared a detailed plan for this college. Vaill lent his approval and spent a long time interviewing prospective students. The collapse of the oil boom and of the Shah's government ended plans for this college and killed any notion of further collaboration with the government of Iran.

In 1976, the school's graduate enrollment stood at an all-time high. In that year, the School of Government and Business Administration enrolled 1,200 master's candidates on campus and 1,100 off campus. That made the program second only to New York University's in enrollment.

By the spring of 1984, the school enrolled one-fourth of the entire student body, a significant increase from the barely 1 percent it registered in the late 1920s. Indeed, by 1984, the school was the second largest undergraduate (1,167 students) division and the largest graduate (2,407 students) division in the entire University.

THE SCHOOL TODAY
In its 1988 form, the school contained six departments—accountancy, business administration, health services administration, management science, public administration, and urban and regional planning.

Each of the departments contained its share of stellar academics. In the field of management science, for example, GW students could benefit from contact with Jerry B. Harvey. Trained in social psychology at the University of Texas, Harvey came to GW in 1971. In his work, he deftly combined insights from the disciplines of psychology and management, and became a major figure in the area of organizational behavior. In the summer of 1974, *Organizational Dynamics* published Harvey's essay on what he described as the "Abilene paradox." This article, since then much discussed and reprinted, explained why groups were unable to work together effectively.

Harvey came to GW in part through the efforts of Gordon Lippitt, who joined the faculty in the 1960s and who was an internationally known expert figure in the field of organizational behavior. Before Lippitt retired in the early 1990s, he published hundreds of articles and 10 books on such topics as leadership, organizations, and group teamwork. He was recognized as one of the outstanding researchers and thinkers in his field.

GW's Department of Public Administration was also among the most distinguished in the nation. The presence of William Adams, an internationally known expert on polling; Kathryn Newcomer, a well-known policy researcher; and Susan Tolchin helped to solidify its reputation. Tolchin, a member of the prestigious National

Academy of Public Administration, wrote a series of well-received books on deregulation and other topics. Many government organizations—the General Accounting Office, as an example— worked closely with Tolchin and the other members of her department in assessing the effectiveness of various programs and agencies.

In addition to the regular degree offerings, the school also continues to run special programs of interest to members of the Washington community, such as the Contemporary Executive Development Program. For the last dozen years, this six-week program has trained senior federal executives in groups of 25 to 40. By now, approximately 1,000 senior executives have benefited from the program.

During the administrations of Deans Peter Vaill, Norma Maine Loeser, and Ben Burdetsky, the transformation from a school of business and public administration to a school of management gradually took place. What one authority describes as an increase in academic competence, research output, and teaching efficiency also occurred in these years. No longer was the school a place where superannuated businessmen or government administrators told war stories to a small number of students. It was instead a vibrant institution in which faculty members skillfully combined educational theory and business practice.

FOWLER

As if to underscore the school's emphasis on management, President Trachtenberg, himself a member of the school's Department of Public Administration, recruited F. David Fowler to become the school's new dean on July 1, 1992. Fowler was a manager as much as he was an academic. In 1963, he began a distinguished career at the accounting firm of Peat Marwick. By 1987, he had worked his way up to become KPMG Peat Marwick's managing partner in the Washington area. In this capacity, he also chaired Peat Marwick International's Personal Development Committee, which was responsible for producing and coordinating professional training programs for member firms around the world. In addition, he directed Peat Marwick's executive education program that delivered programs generating some $6 million in revenue annually. A man of widely ranging interests, Fowler provided oversight for a consulting team that prepared a strategic plan for the D.C. public schools in the 1990s. He later became chair of the D.C. Committee on Public Education and testified frequently before Congress on educational issues.

At GW, Fowler put his background in management and management training to work. A former director of Peat Marwick's philanthropic foundation, he extended the school's outreach to the area's corporate and private foundations. He used his business connections to secure challenging internships for GW students and to bring leading business executives to campus. He showed that a person with the right skills could make the transition from the worlds of business and administration to the field of education. Fowler proved to be superbly qualified to lead a school dedicated, as Burdetsky had put it, to teaching students how to be more effective managers.

Rodney Patterson, School of Business and Public Management alumnus (B.B.A. '93, M.B.A. '95) and former Colonials basketball player, received the Courage Award from President Bill Clinton in 1994. Patterson, diagnosed with lymphoma in 1991, fought back after treatment to return to the court for the end of his senior year.

(Left) Students attend a concert in the University Yard at the Program Board's Fall Fest 1993.

(Right) Throughout GW's history, students have enjoyed festive activities on the University Yard.

Continued from p. 162

STUDENT LIFE IN THE 1980S

When the report was released, GW students were nearly a generation removed from the activism of the late 1960s and early 1970s. Thurston Hall, the superdorm, still housed the most students of any dorm on campus. It no longer had the reputation as the "zoo," a place of "unending chaos, excitement, noise, people, and frustration." Instead, one resident-assistant pointed to its many advantages, including the cafeteria located in the basement and computer, typing and piano rooms. Furthermore, Thurston's rooms had air conditioning and their own bathrooms, not to mention a weekly cleaning service. It was a far cry from a Spartan setting for a student, who might well come to school equipped with a personal computer and a VCR.

And, in true GW style, residence in Thurston brought the GW student flush up against the Washington scene, since the Embassy of Uruguay was located only a door away. In earlier times, there had been some friction between the dorm and the embassy. In 1971, Thurston residents, all of whom were female, stitched together some bedsheets and made a protest banner, which they hung outside of the dorm. The banner apparently depicted the male sex organ, a fact not well received by the diplomats in the embassy. Occasionally, too, undergraduate exuberance led to streamers of toilet paper being inadvertently hung from one of the trees on embassy property.

Just as Thurston became a co-ed dormitory, so did nearly all of the other GW residential facilities. In 1987, Calhoun Hall, soon to be renamed Adams Hall, became one of the last to go co-ed. Forty-two men lived on the seventh and eighth floors. On the other floors, women were in the majority.

When these men and women went out on the town, they often traveled across Pennsylvania Avenue and took in a movie at the Circle Theater. In 1957, while Jim and Ted Pedas were still students at GW's law school, they bought the theater, one of Washington's oldest. After an initial flop with conventional programming, they decided to show a repertory of old classics. Prices were kept low. Until the theater closed in 1986, GW students flocked to the Circle to see such movies as *Casablanca*, *Citizen Kane*, and *The Philadelphia Story*.

When Jesse Jackson spoke at Lisner Auditorium in September 1985, he drew an audience of only 1,000. The relatively low turn-out demonstrated that GW students of the 1980s were more conservative than those of the 1970s. These students, attending college in the era of Ronald Reagan, helped to revive the Greek system.

The fraternities and sororities of the 1980s prided themselves on their social services and academic support services. To be a member of Delta Tau Delta, for example, one had to maintain at least a 2.25 grade point average. Kappa Sigma pledges helped to start a chapter on the Gallaudet University campus and raised money for the cause of muscular dystrophy research. The brothers of Zeta Beta Tau participated in blood drives and served food at Miriam's Kitchen, which fed hundreds of homeless citizens every week.

To cope with the rising interest in fraternities and sororities, the University appointed a Greek Affairs coordinator. By 1985, most of the campus leadership belonged to one of the houses. Together, the fraternities and sororities raised more than $12,000 for charities and as *The Hatchet* rather grudgingly admitted, "(they) are doing some positive things for the campus."

THE VIRGINIA CAMPUS

The Commission on the Year 2000 included, among its many recommendations, a suggestion that the University should acquire land in a suburban location "to give the institution flexibility in developing future research and instruction opportunities." On May 15, 1986, President Elliott made an announcement to the Board of Trustees that he called "very important for the University's history." Through the generosity of Trustee Robert Smith, the University had received a gift of 50 acres, located in Loudoun County, Virginia, near Dulles Airport, from the Washington Engineering Associates Limited Partnership. The land formed part of a larger parcel that was to be developed into a major research and development park.

On this property the University hoped to consolidate several off-campus programs—it already enrolled over 2,000 students in off-campus programs at some 65 sites across the Metropolitan area—and to develop facilities for research that could not be done on the Foggy Bottom campus. Unlike other schools, GW had no industrial base to support research. The new center in Northern Virginia would put GW in close proximity to scores of large firms and high-tech companies and enable the University to conduct research in collaboration with those firms.

(Above) GW broke ground on its Virginia Campus on July 16, 1990, in Loudoun County, Va.

(Right) In 1991, a new 71,000 square-foot research and class-room building occupied the Loudoun County site. The University began to offer 14 graduate programs and more than 30 non-degree professional advancement courses at the location.

The University devoted the next years to planning the Virginia Campus. In January 1989, a task force, led by Vice President French, received the charge of developing a strategic plan for the new campus. This task force decided that the University should offer degrees in engineering and applied science, government and business administration, and education and human development at the center. The center might, for example, house programs leading to an executive M.B.A., a Ph.D. (or master's) in computer science, to an advanced degree in electrical engineering, or a doctorate in education in the field of human resource development. The task force defined computer science, operations research, electromagnetics, and communications as research priorities for the center.

What Lloyd Elliott had begun, Stephen Joel Trachtenberg brought to reality when, on July 16, 1990, he presided at the groundbreaking in Virginia. Two hundred people attended the ceremony. In 1991, a new 71,000 square-foot research and classroom building occupied the Loudoun County site. The University began to offer 14 graduate programs and more than 30 non-degree professional advancement courses at the location. Research and development offices, including those of the Melpar Division of E-Systems, took shape around the new building.

In this way, without in any manner disturbing the arrangement of the Foggy Bottom campus, the University expanded to Virginia. As one prominent University official put it, "Thirty or 40 years ago, the idea that an academic campus could be so interwoven with the needs of the business world and the greater community might have been greeted with actual horror. But, in the America of 1990, it not only makes good sense, but perfect sense."

The initiation of planning for the Virginia campus marked one of Lloyd Elliott's last major acts as GW president. By 1987, people had begun to bandy about the phrase, "Harvard on the Potomac." Elliott himself disliked the expression. GW would never be Harvard. It would instead be a university that continued to take advantage of its special location. Elliott cited the linkages between the law school and the many private firms and government agencies engaged in legal work. He also mentioned GW's programs with the Smithsonian, the National Gallery, and the National Institute of Standards and Technology. Notable scholarship was produced through collaborative efforts such as these. In 1988, Anthropology Professor Alison S. Brooks led a GW/National Science Foundation scientific team to Zaire; that dig unearthed tools that later proved to predate European tools of similar design by some 75,000 years. Another example is the relationship between English Professor Gail Kern Paster, who has authored two books on Elizabethan theatre, and the Folger Shakespeare Library. Numerous similar situations have existed through the years and are ongoing.

In the spring of 1987, Lloyd Elliott announced that he would retire on June 30, 1988. Asked to cite his major accomplishments, he said, "We've appointed a dozen or more distinguished professors in the last five years whom we never would have been able to get in 1965. We're able to match their salaries at Illinois and Yale and places like that." He also mentioned that the "medical and law schools have moved forward very rapidly and the engineering school now ranks among the best in the country in terms of research funds per professor."

Perhaps Rod French put it best when he wrote that, "It has been the great good fortune of The George Washington University to have had Lloyd Elliott as president in this quarter century when the emergence of Washington as an international capital of culture and economics, as well as of politics, has hugely escalated the demands of the calling to be a great Washington university." Elliott turned GW not into Harvard, but into a great Washington university, with research and teaching capabilities that far surpassed those of the Marvin era.

BUSINESS EXTRA

The Boston G

Vol. 219, No. 90© 1981, Globe Newspaper Co. *

TUESDAY, MARCH 31, 1981

REAGAN SHOT; CO
IS 'GOOD' AFTER S

shots rang out on sidewalk outside Washington Hilton Hotel, President Reagan was shoved through the rear door of his limousine by alert Secre

ust who
was in
harge?

P
2

lobe

Light of day
TUESDAY — Partly sunny, near 70
WEDNESDAY — Clouds, windy, 70s
HIGH TIDE — 7:07 a.m., 7:44 p.m.
FULL REPORT — PAGE 60

Telephone 929-2000 | Classified Circulation 929-1500 929-2222 | 60 Pages – 25 Cents

NDITION

URGERY

vice agents. Limousine sped President to hospital. AP PHOTO

ess secretary Brady,
thers also

A Campus
Transformed

(Left) Stephen Joel Trachtenberg became the 15th president of The George Washington University on August 1, 1988.

(Above) On the way to his first opening convocation as GW president, President Trachtenberg stopped to say hello to a group of local children playing on campus.

STEPHEN JOEL TRACHTENBERG

The University moved quickly to hire the next president. On January 21, 1988, came the announcement that Stephen Joel Trachtenberg, the president of the University of Hartford, would succeed Lloyd Elliott. He arrived on campus in August 1988.

Trachtenberg became only GW's fourth president since 1927. Unlike any of his predecessors, he was Jewish, the son of Russian immigrants from Odessa. Born in 1937, he grew up in Brooklyn, New York. His parents demanded that he do well in school, and he responded positively to the pressure. He recalled that his parents "had a notion of the world as a dog-eat-dog competitive place...and the key to getting through was being elected to the academic honor society. It was a secular religion called education."

Young Trachtenberg practiced this religion with great enthusiasm. After he graduated from James Madison High School in 1955, he went to Columbia University. From there he took a law degree at

Yale. Already he had transcended the boundaries of his insurance agent father's world. With his prestigious degree, he secured a job as an attorney in the New York office of the Atomic Energy Commission, where he spent three years.

He enjoyed the work until he perceived that it was too repetitive to hold his interest over the course of a lifetime. He turned toward the world of Washington, working first as an aide to John Brademas, the Indiana congressman and future university president (NYU) who played a key role in the passage of Great Society education legislation. In 1966, Trachtenberg became a special assistant to Harold "Doc" Howe, the United States education commissioner. Along the way he studied at what became the Kennedy School at Harvard, earning a Master's in Public Administration.

Not long after Richard Nixon won the 1968 election, Trachtenberg moved to Boston University, where he performed a variety of administrative jobs for the next eight years. Trachtenberg arrived under the aegis of Calvin Lee, who ran the College of Liberal Arts. Soon, however, he had to contend with John Silber, who, within a few short years of coming to Boston University, became one of the most famous college presidents in America. Trachtenberg developed a rapport with the often contentious Silber, who thought highly enough of Trachtenberg to appoint him acting dean of arts and sciences and dean of university affairs. Silber later described Trachtenberg as "caring and daring and truly dynamic."

With his appointment at Hartford in 1977, Trachtenberg made the leap into the ranks of college presidents. He proceeded to consolidate the academic and financial fortunes of that struggling school, turning it into a highly regarded regional university. Although he enjoyed himself immensely, he decided that he was not completely defined by his experience. When the call came from George Washington, he was "wary about returning to Washington for the third time in my career, but I also felt I had to try it, to test myself."

THE TRACHTENBERG ERA BEGINS

With characteristic energy, President Trachtenberg plunged into his work at George Washington. Although Lloyd Elliott had run the school with a firm hand, he had never called attention to himself. From the beginning, Trachtenberg made the GW presidency a more personal office, and, like Cloyd Marvin in earlier times, he took an interest in nearly all aspects of the University. As he described the

Rep. John Lewis of Georgia (l) and Yolanda King (r) were among five human rights activists, including one GW student, who received GW's Dr. Martin Luther King Jr. Medal from President Trachtenberg (center) at the University's "The Dream in Action" convocation on January 24, 1994.

U.S. Housing and Urban Development Secretary and GW alumnus Henry Cisneros (D.P.A. '76) came to campus to discuss empowerment zones and enterprise communities at a conference sponsored by GW's Department of Public Administration in 1994.

(Right) Alumnus and Chairman of the Joint Chiefs of Staff Gen. John Shalikashvili (M.S. '70) was awarded GW's Distinguished Alumni Achievement Award in 1993. He is shown here with former Elliott School of International Affairs Dean Maurice East (left) and President Trachtenberg.

situation, "GW can probably float for 10 years and I can retire to Palm Springs and then I can have generations of faculty and administrators curse my name because I left them in bad shape."

Trachtenberg did not intend for that to happen. Instead he promised that within 10 years, George Washington would be "unquestionably the best university in the District of Columbia, one of the pre-eminent institutions in this part of the country, an institution recognized nationally and internationally as the premier place to come in certain disciplines and a good place to come in all the disciplines that it offers."

Like his predecessors, President Trachtenberg quickly came to realize that the University's location conferred certain advantages and disadvantages upon it. In contrast to Hartford, no corporate elite guided the educational and philanthropic fortunes of Washington, D.C. At the same time, the University enjoyed one of the most enviable locations in the nation. "For this university not to constantly have on its mind the fact that it's in Washington, two blocks from the State Department, would be lunacy," Trachtenberg said. "This is not the University that's going to develop the cure for some wheat malady," he added. "This is an institution that can make major contributions in all kinds of public policy areas."

As Trachtenberg understood, much of the Washington community already owed a considerable debt to GW. All of the branches of the federal government boasted GW alumni among their leaders. One example, among many that could be cited, was the military's Joint Chiefs of Staff. Three of the recent chairmen (Generals Vessey, Powell, and Shalikashvili) studied at GW.

(Left) The Rev. Jesse Jackson, a shadow senator for the District of Columbia, voiced his support of D.C. statehood at the "A Time of Change" national conference in the Marvin Center in 1993. The conference examined the relationship between the United States and its territories.

(Below) After attending a performance of the Ballet Folklorico de Mexico at Lisner Auditorium in 1991, President and Mrs. George Bush received a Mexican folk mask in the Dimock Gallery from members of the dance company.

The Trachtenberg era began formally in April 1989 with his inauguration as University president. The new president believed in pomp and circumstance, if only to send a message that GW deserved to call attention to itself. As he put it, "The George Washington University is one of the best kept secrets in American higher education...The George Washington University needs to love itself more." In this manner, the Trachtenberg inauguration became a chance for the University to celebrate what was best about itself. Speaking on what he called "the single most important day of my professional life," Trachtenberg described the University as a "force within American higher education now and in the future." "My role," he said, "is to point out to people what a wonderful place it really is."

GW AS NATIONAL CENTER

The University achieved a new level of visibility under President Trachtenberg, both in the community and in the nation. The new president built on his predecessor's outreach to the community, inaugurating a generous scholarship program to outstanding D.C. high school graduates, frequently attending churches with primarily African-American members, and regularly interacting with Mayors Kelly and Barry.

In June 1990, the Smith Center served as the international press center for American and foreign journalists covering the Bush-Gorbachev summit. On this occasion, Secretary of State James

Baker appeared, and White House Press Secretary Marlin Fitzwater briefed an estimated 5,000 correspondents daily. The situation required that 900 additional phone lines be installed in the Smith Center. AT&T logged a daily average of 3,000 long distance phone calls.

With careful attention to detail, GW assisted in this massive effort. It provided a Summit Minimart at the bookstore, with supplies for the journalists such as Maalox and extra-strength Tylenol.

In 1991, the president announced that Ronald Reagan would receive an honorary degree on March 28 on the occasion of the tenth anniversary of his life-saving surgery at the Medical Center. On that date, the University also unveiled a plaque honoring Nancy Reagan's courage and strength during her husband's hospitalization. In addition, the University established the Ronald Reagan Institute of Emergency Medicine. When Reagan came to GW, it marked only his second visit back to the city since his presidency. He used the opportunity to announce his support for the Brady handgun control bill, a major endorsement for the bill's proponents.

The 1993 change in presidential administration brought even more traffic between GW and the White House. For example, when Hillary Rodham Clinton sought a venue to discuss her health care reform plan in 1993, she chose GW.

(Right) Secretary of State James A. Baker III addressed the media in the Smith Center during the Bush-Gorbachev summit in June 1990.

(Far right) President Ronald Reagan returned to GW to accept an honorary degree in 1991—10 years after his life-saving treatment at the GW Hospital following an assassination attempt.

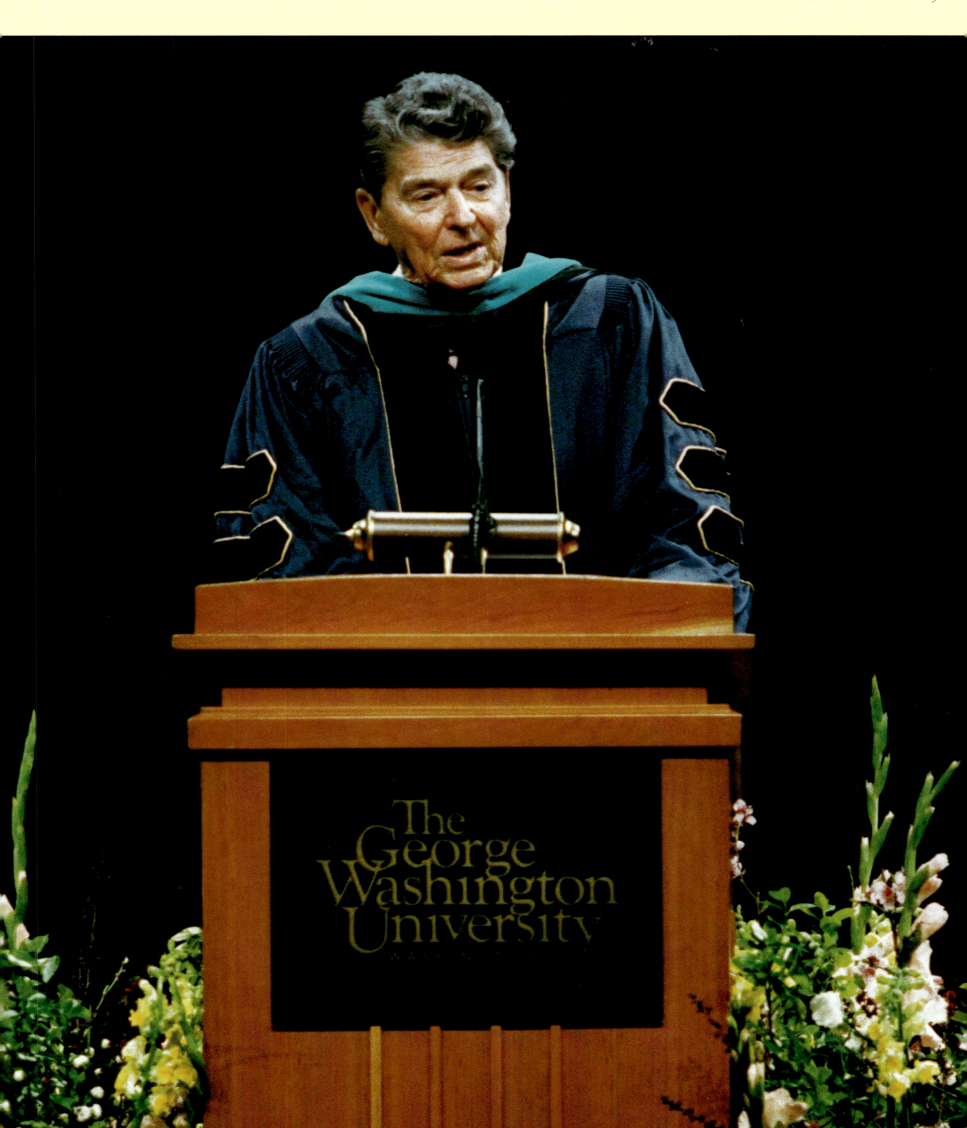

Encouraging this sort of link between the University and the conduct of the nation's public policy became a hallmark of the Trachtenberg presidency. Along with other University leaders, the president entertained the idea of creating a central focus on policy issues, interdisciplinary in nature, dedicated to research—and yet attentive to the University's educational programs.

The University had gone down this road before. A start-up grant from NASA in 1967 had produced a policy studies unit that proved unequal to the task of assembling the teams of scholars who had been expected to attract major funding and make major contributions to national debates on policy issues. This unit boosted the highly successful program in science and technology policy, but it failed to realize the comprehensive, integrative vision that inspired its creation. When GW's first and only vice president for policy studies retired in 1982, the unit, but not the vision, died.

Less encompassing efforts kept policy studies alive. Starting with an educational policy program in the early 1970s, Dean Henry Solomon's subsequent leadership expanded the graduate school's aegis over policy studies to six doctoral fields and three thematic master's degree programs. In addition, by 1990 GW boasted a new Center for Health Policy Research. The three units together constituted one of the major university-based health policy clusters in the nation. The center complemented the work of Judith Miller Jones, whose National Health Policy Forum disseminated information on significant health issues to key decision makers on Capitol Hill and other prominent locations, and that of Richard Merritt, whose Intergovernmental Health Policy Project performed a similar function for state government.

All in all, when President Trachtenberg arrived, the University already had a stunning assemblage of first-class programs of research and instruction on public policy, some of them department-based, others bringing a range of disciplines sharply to bear on particular policy questions. Putting together efforts in the closely related but differentiable fields of public affairs, public administration, and just plain government would be President Trachtenberg's goal. He proceeded to charge the University's policy scholars to reinvent at GW the study of the management of public life. He challenged them to create a congenial new structure for conducting research, consulting, presenting vigorous degree programs, hosting visiting scholars, and offering short courses, conferences, seminars, and workshops on public policy issues. In this manner, Trachtenberg moved to close the gap between the University's performance and its potential for superb achievement in this vital area of scholarship and teaching.

President of the Czech Republic Václav Havel received the President's Medal from GW on April 22, 1993. Havel, the University's first recipient of the medal, was honored for his efforts to help bring about the downfall of communism in the former Czechoslovakia.

Renowned journalist Walter Cronkite came to campus in 1994 to discuss issues that have shaped global alliances and conflicts since World War II. He is shown here with GW Vice President for Administrative and Information Services Walter Bortz.

(Left) Health and Human Services Secretary Donna Shalala and Vice President Al Gore, among others, listened to concerns regarding health care at the first public meeting of President Clinton's Task Force for National Health Care on March 29, 1993, held in the Smith Center.

(Right) On Community Service Day, more than 1,000 freshmen volunteered at various sites across the city of Washington. This group of students gathered trash from the banks of the Anacostia River.

In a related move in 1990, Trachtenberg encouraged the young, New York-based Graduate School of Political Management to relocate to GW's campus. The Graduate School of Political Management offered courses in election management, government representation and lobbying, issue advocacy, law, and political leadership, all leading to a Master's of Professional Studies in Political Management. Each of these programs and majors united academic ideas and practical experience; each benefited from the intellectual environment of Columbian College and the Graduate School of Arts and Sciences. The founding president of the school agreed with President Trachtenberg that the program belonged in Washington and that the education of students in this new career path would be enriched by a closer affiliation with a comprehensive university. In the spring of 1995, the Board of Trustees voted to assimilate the Graduate School of Political Management as fully a part of the University.

An area of particular concern for President Trachtenberg was the environment. On December 12, 1994, Trachtenberg and Environmental Protection Agency Administrator Carol Browner officially signed a landmark agreement to create the nation's first model "Green University." Through this agreement, GW became the only institution of higher learning in the world that was committed to becoming totally "green." "I want to commend the University for being a leader," said EPA Administrator Browner, "and look forward to seeing many other colleges and universities learn from this ground-breaking agreement and follow the lead of this trail-blazing institution."

At the signing ceremony, Trachtenberg noted that GW's actions would have a major impact upon the city, the region, and the University itself. He emphasized that GW was a "multi-campus institution with considerable additional development both underway and planned." He pointed out that the University was the District of Columbia's largest private-sector employer, using the

(Left) During Earth Week 1994, John Von Kerens, assistant director for grounds, transportation, and housekeeping, participated in a tree planting ceremony.

(Above) Vice President Al Gore gave a major speech on the environment and climate control on March 17, 1995, in the Marvin Theatre.

(Below) President Trachtenberg and Environmental Protection Agency Administrator Carol Browner signed a landmark agreement to create the nation's first model "Green University" on December 12, 1994.

services of more than 26,000 vendors each year and making a huge impact on the regional economy. From GW's point of view, the president said that the agreement was "just plain good business," one that would give the University "a competitive advantage in today's educational, research, and health care marketplaces by strengthening our attractiveness in recruiting, marketing, and sales efforts; conserving precious natural resources; cutting down our energy consumption; and reducing our operating expenses."

As part of GW's "Green University" initiative, the University established an Institute for the Environment that cut across the various colleges and schools. As with policy studies, the president wanted "to fully integrate this greening effort into our management and operations." He realized that GW already had a solid foundation of environmental activities on which to build. It consisted, among other things, of 100 courses related to the environment that spanned six degree programs. It was the president's strong desire and a key test of his leadership to bring these courses and programs together. The result would be, as the agreement with the EPA stated, that GW would "incorporate a strong, environmentally conscientious ethic

The George
Washington
University
WASHINGTON DC

(Left) Senior Clinton Advisor George Stephanopoulos held a televised press conference in the Marvin Theatre on Jan. 19, 1993, as part of Bill Clinton's presidential inauguration preparations.

(Below) Noted journalist Marvin Kalb hosted a televised series of political discussions known as "The Kalb Report," produced by GW and the National Press Club.

into all of its activities" and "actively promote the principles of environmental sustainability in its management and operations." If President Trachtenberg realized his vision, then the University would produce graduates who would "reflect an unwavering commitment to create and lead us on paths to environmental and economic sustainability." Through the "Green University" initiative, the University would foster environmental leadership and stewardship.

GW in the Trachtenberg era became an important intersection of press and politics. In January 1993, GW served as the Clinton-Gore Inaugural Press Center, hosting 800 visiting journalists as well as the inaugural committee press office and transition team communications operation. Four hundred GW students served as volunteers during this two-week period. The Dorothy Betts Marvin Theatre served as the site of 14 press briefings in 12 days, many of which were carried live by major radio and television networks.

This effort served as a catalyst for expanded relations between GW and journalists worldwide. It also laid the foundation for GW's successes as host site for such network broadcasts as CNN "Crossfire" and the William F. Buckley "Firing Line" debates. And, in an unprecedented alliance, GW and the National Press Club joined

forces to produce the nationally broadcast series, "The Kalb Report: Public Policy and the Press," moderated by former CBS chief diplomatic correspondent and GW visiting professor Marvin Kalb.

The establishment of the National Center for Communication Studies (NCCS) was a major project of the Trachtenberg presidency. Here again, the president displayed his penchant for uniting previously disparate activities and creating a synergism that strengthened the University. In this case, President Trachtenberg helped to establish the NCCS as a sort of school within a school by merging the Departments of Communication and Journalism with the Political Communication Program. The center began operations on July 1, 1991.

The NCCS offers undergraduate degrees that give students a solid grounding in the traditional liberal arts curriculum and that allow them a chance to learn about the high-tech world of communications. The Political Communication Program provides the nation's first undergraduate degree in that subject. Students in this highly popular program explore such topics as the role of journalists in the political system, the development and effectiveness of communication strategies in political campaigns, communication patterns and issues in international relations, and the functions of communication in the political lives of contemporary societies.

Continued on p. 197

(Above) The blue clock next to the Gelman Library was part of President Trachtenberg's campus beautification plan, which also included distinctive GW banners and flower beds dotting the campus.

(Below) Between classes, students enjoy lunchtime at "J Street," the Marvin Center's new food court approach to feeding hungry students.

The Faculty Senate

A forum, a sounding-board, a policy-maker, a governing body, an instrument of "faculty power," or a waster of time—in all of these guises the Faculty Senate appears in the minds of the professoriate, depending on its mood and the issue at hand.

For nearly 35 years, senate members (not properly referred to as senators) have met monthly to consider the state of academe. Here, as their charge prescribes, they mull over resolutions affecting "more than one school." Sometimes they correct a hitherto unnoticed flaw in the faculty's collective enterprise. More often, they pick up on some all-too-apparent flaw in the administration's conduct. Members also routinely and sometimes vociferously advise the president who is suffered (and sometimes suffers) to preside over their meetings. They also read tributes to colleagues who have died, defend tenure when they think it threatened, urge higher salaries and greater medical benefits, and occasionally tinker with the University calendar. Their most sustained activity, however, has been to tell the administration how much better things would be if their advice were taken. All this proceeds, observers note, whether the issue is great or small, with a stiff formality that even an ebullient Stephen Joel Trachtenberg has difficulty cracking.

Art Professor Lilien Robinson (left) has been a Faculty Senate member for 17 years; she was chair of the executive committee for five years.

Today's Faculty Senate draws its structure from the Faculty Organization Plan, adopted in 1961. But it drew its original inspiration from an insistence, cresting in the late 1950s, that faculty be consulted on all matters that touched their professional lives. From its inception, the plan, and with it the Faculty Code, have spoken to the faculty's firm belief that they are co-managers of the academic enterprise, not simply its hired hands.

By way of background, President Cloyd Heck Marvin's penchant for "running everything" had given faculty little opportunity to express themselves. By

Romance Languages Professor Yvonne Captain became a member of the Faculty Senate Executive Committee in 1995.

1959, the year Marvin retired, their mood was sullenly rebellious. As the late Howard Merriman, one of the plan's authors, put it, "We were tired of the way Marvin ran things." His colleague, the late Wood Gray, put it more bluntly. Marvin, he often said, could only be described as a "benevolent despot," whose departure in January 1959 set in train the liberating events of the next two years.

The plan began to take shape when faculty met in what Professor Emeritus Roderic Davison remembers as "the largest faculty meeting I ever saw at GW." Gathered in Lisner Auditorium in the fall of 1959, they overwhelmingly adopted Professor Fred Sailsbury Tupper's rather vague resolution to create a committee that would determine the faculty's role in the future of the University. Although the Committee of Eighteen, as it was called, began at once to draft the plan, nearly two years passed before the senate became a reality.

Delays resulted not so much from obstructionism as from the erratic tempo of academic life. Acting President Oswald Colclough offered neither encouragement nor opposition. The trustees, according to Merriman, evinced no interest whatever. The Committee of Eighteen, meanwhile, busied itself that

fall and winter, scrupulously canvassing all nine schools for ideas while at the same time relying for counsel on the American Association of University Professors. By spring 1960, the committee had produced a draft charter that it submitted to Colclough for his "advice." The acting president, clearly taking a neutral position, made only a few suggestions, and then left for a junket to Europe. By the time the faculty had approved a revised draft in late April, it was too late for the trustees' meeting in May.

When classes resumed in the fall, Colclough nudged the process along by appointing a "temporary organizing committee," which, in turn, drafted "temporary bylaws." The president was still on hand when the senate held its first meeting on January 13, 1961. In March, faculty were pleased to note that the newly installed president, Thomas Carroll, was quick to give the undertaking his blessing as he opened the senate's third meeting. Fortunately, Carroll had had experience with faculty governance elsewhere and, although his relations with the fledgling body were often tense (which may explain its lasting formality), he left Lloyd Elliott with what had become a fully-accepted consultative body.

One of the senate's earliest achievements was its drafting of the Faculty Code. The code has done for faculty rights what the organization plan did for faculty structure: consecrated them both in writing. Although a reading of the code may hide the fact that it protects the broad concept of "academic freedom" in tightly written, legal-sounding language, the most detailed and delicate relationships that divide faculty from administration are spelled out. What the senate created, it has always staunchly defended, although sometimes seemingly ill-armed and sometimes outmatched.

At base, the power of the senate has always been the power of a good argument. Its resolutions are not mandates. Rather, they take the form of recommendations to the president, who may accept or reject, but, if the latter, the senate expects an explanation. Where conflict most often arises is over whether the faculty has truly been consulted. Is it enough that the faculty be notified and its counter-arguments heard? Or should faculty input be determinative? Along the thin edge of these opposing views, senate debate is often lively.

The senate's influence also owes much to its Executive Committee whose carefully selected chairs have combined watchfulness with the studied avoidance of an "us vs. them" mindset. In preferring cooperation to confrontation—except in the direst circumstances—chairs like Professors John Morgan,

Lilien Robinson, and William Griffith, to mention the most recent, have consistently succeeded in winning both the confidence of the administration and the support of their constituents. Griffith, who served two three-year terms under Presidents Elliott and Trachtenberg, sees a continuity in the senate's usefulness to both parties. On one hand, it shoulders the faculty's responsibility for guiding institutional policies and for defining the University's mission. On the other hand, it puts the administration on notice, says Griffith, that "GW can't be run entirely from the top down. The administration has to bring the faculty along if it wants its policies to be successful."

Philosophy Professor William Griffith, a member of the Faculty Senate for 20 years, served six years as chair of the executive committee.

Continued from p. 192

The founding of the NCCS helped to rejuvenate each of its constituent entities, such as the Radio and Television Program, which had begun in the late 1940s with an emphasis on radio and had expanded to a full degree program covering all electronic media in 1979.

Through the NCCS, therefore, The George Washington University played a leadership role, in the context of the nation's capital, in educational, creative, and scholarly activities related to the study of communication. Students benefited not only from exposure to such leading scholars as Chris Sterling, author of *Broadcasting in America*, a standard treatise in its field that has gone through eight editions, and Jarol Manheim, author of *Strategic Public Diplomacy and American Foreign Policy: The Evolution of Influence*, but also from frequent encounters with the leading practitioners in the field. The students in Charles Puffenbarger's journalism class, for example, visited newsrooms at *USA Today*, the Associated Press, and the Hearst Washington Bureau, and heard informal lectures by reporters from *The Washington Post*, *The Baltimore Sun*, and *Time*.

The center has become the editorial home of *Journalism Quarterly*, the leading scholarly journal in the field edited by journalism Professor Jean Folkerts. It also has received significant external funding, such as from the AT&T Foundation, which gave a grant to the center for a scholars-in-residence program and an international communication forum series. The NCCS figures to be an important part of GW's future and an enduring legacy of the Trachtenberg years.

In addition to attending to these major initiatives, the president invested time and energy in improving GW's appearance. Flower beds bloomed across the campus. Residence halls and other buildings received distinctive banners that announced their presence and brought a sense of architectural unity to the campus. An ornate clock appeared next to the library, and one could often spot an English double-decker bus parked in front of the Marvin Center, ready to show off the campus and environs to prospective students.

(Left) Students take a study break on the University Yard.

(Right) With more than 200 registered student organizations on campus, festivities abound throughout the year.

(Below) Computers have become as much a part of classrooms as chalk boards and pencils.

Gone were the days of utilitarian architecture and classrooms painted Marvin green. The campus had acquired a sense of style that was evident in everything from the graceful design of the trash cans in public areas, to the appealing layout of the "J Street" cafes in the Marvin Center, to the newly refurbished lecture facility in Funger Hall.

To transform the campus into an aesthetically pleasing and more functional entity, President Trachtenberg put in place both a master construction plan and an amenities plan to deal with outside spaces. Among the major new initiatives was a large dormitory, slated to be built at 24th and H Streets. It would provide its residents with what planners described as "apartment living."

At 23rd and G Streets, the University contemplated the creation of a health and wellness center, a gym designed not for athletic competition so much as for personal fitness. It would contain such features as basketball courts, squash courts, running tracks, a weight room, and even a juice bar. In a sense, it would give members of the University community their own personal health club and contribute to the community's general fitness and tone.

The University also made a vigorous effort to tone up the many townhouses and other Foggy Bottom buildings that GW owned. In the process, it provided new homes for such important campus organizations at *The Hatchet* and for programs such as the undergraduate Honors Program. Indeed, the Trachtenberg years saw a

(Left) In 1994, GW transformed a classroom in Funger Hall into a state-of-the-art lecture hall. Shown, center, Sharon Confessore, an assistant professor in the Graduate School of Education and Human Development, advises students after class.

(Top) Quigley's Pharmacy, which now houses the geography department, was a popular gathering place for students in earlier years.

(Below) A view toward Gelman Library on H Street from the Academic Center breezeway.

(Left) President Trachtenberg welcomes a group of GW's incoming 1994 "21st Century Scholars"—outstanding D.C. public school graduates on full, four-year GW scholarships.

(Right) President Bill Clinton and his daughter, Chelsea, and her friend joined GW President Trachtenberg, his wife, Francine, and his son, Ben, in the Smith Center for the GW v. U. Mass. basketball game on February 4, 1995. GW defeated U. Mass., 78-75.

major expansion of this program. Another important rehabilitation project involved the former University Inn, which in fall 1994 became the home of the Graduate School of Education and Human Development. In a sense, the University rebuilt the entire building, at a cost of some $3 million, and created what amounted to a new facility.

As the experience with the Honors Program demonstrated, the University did far more than sell the sizzle. Much more importantly, it attracted the best students in the University's history to its campus. A concerted effort began to attract National Merit Scholars and others of superior achievement to GW. Beginning in 1991, the effort paid off handsomely, as the increasing college board scores of the entering freshmen demonstrated. "We are going after the best students," the president noted. The fact that of the 1,192 members of the 1995 freshman class, 39 percent were in the top 10 percent of their high school class, showed that it was getting many of them. In 1993, GW attracted the largest freshman class in its history, a vote of confidence in GW and a GW education. In 1995, GW received more than 10,000 applications from prospective undergraduates, something that had never happened before and further proof of the University's rising quality.

These students who came to GW in the Trachtenberg era demonstrated a level of school spirit that was unprecedented in GW's recent history. These were students who combined a '90s sensibility, with its attendant concern for such social issues as saving the environment and helping the homeless, and an old-fashioned sense of school pride. Suddenly it became fashionable to attend sporting events and to wear clothes that prominently featured the GW logo.

It helped in this regard that President Trachtenberg was himself a devoted fan of GW's athletic and other endeavors. One enduring image of Trachtenberg's presidency featured a picture of the president and his family watching GW play basketball in the Smith Center against the University of Massachusetts. Next to Trachtenberg, his wife, and son, Ben, sat another avid basketball fan, who had decided to take time off from his own presidential duties and enjoy the game with his daughter, Chelsea. On this occasion, GW defeated a team that at the time was ranked number one in the nation.

PLAYING ABOVE THE RIM

President Trachtenberg realized that he was only as good as the team around him. For that reason, he paid particular attention to selecting the deans of the various schools. Among those who came to GW during Trachtenberg's era was Jack Friedenthal, who moved from Stanford to take over the law school and accelerate its rise to prominence. Linda Bradley Salamon arrived from Washington University in St. Louis and proceeded to raise the academic standards and intellectual aspirations of the newly united Columbian College and Graduate School of Arts and Sciences (subsequently renamed, in July 1995, "Columbian School of Arts and Sciences"). An intensive national search yielded Harry Harding, a distinguished scholar of Chinese history and politics at the Brookings Institution, as the dean of what was now known, appropriately, as

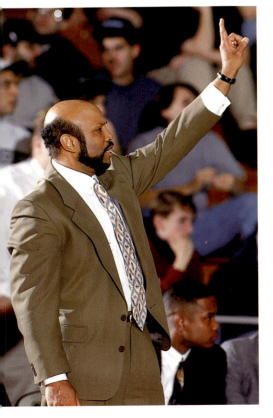

(Left) Mike Jarvis, head men's basketball coach, turned around the men's basketball program at GW. Two years before Jarvis came to GW, the team won only one of its 28 games for the season.

(Above) Men's basketball took a giant leap forward during the 1990s, twice earning invitations to NCAA post-season tournaments and qualifying for Sweet Sixteen play in 1993.

(Right) Women's volleyball team in action; the team won Atlantic 10 championships in 1993 and in 1994.

Men's sports at GW today include baseball, basketball, crew, cross-country, golf, soccer, swimming and diving, tennis, and water polo.

GW fields women's teams in basketball, crew, cross-country, gymnastics, soccer, swimming and diving, tennis, and volleyball.

the Elliott School of International Affairs. Dean F. David Fowler lent his extensive business experience to the School of Business and Public Management. Dean Gideon Frieder supplied firm guidance to the School of Engineering and Applied Science.

Trachtenberg also knew that GW's spirit, morale, and image would benefit from the presence of winning sports teams. In May 1990, the fortunes of the men's basketball team, a once and future source of glory, improved upon the arrival of Mike Jarvis as the head coach. As he had done at Boston University, Jarvis turned the GW program around. In 1992, the team's prospects brightened further with the addition of Yinka Dare to the GW squad. In 1993, the GW basketball team, led by Dare, made an improbable appearance in the round of 16 at the NCAA tournament. The team came close to beating the University of Michigan and pulling off what would have been one of the greatest upsets in tournament history. The next year the team once again appeared in the NCAA tournament, a considerable accomplishment when one considered that GW had made only two previous NCAA tournament appearances in the entire history of its basketball program.

Not only the men's basketball team, but many other GW teams fared well in the 1990s. The women's basketball program acquired national prominence, and the team often ranked among the top 20 teams in the nation. The soccer, gymnastics, and volleyball teams also grew in stature and excellence.

Success in athletics confirmed the wisdom of the University's strategy of promoting sports without sacrificing academic quality. In this regard, President Trachtenberg fully agreed with President Elliott's earlier decision not to continue competing in intercollegiate football. Among other things, the presence of a football program would upset the gender equity that prevailed among GW sports programs.

Nothing showed the University to better advantage than its ceremonial events. On May 8, 1994, Hillary Rodham Clinton delivered

the principal address at GW's commencement. The day had dawned chilly and gray. As the ceremonies began, the sun appeared from behind the clouds, adding a note of optimism to what was already a festive event. The ceremony took place on the Ellipse, directly in back of the White House. Representatives of each of the University's schools were in attendance.

The first lady reminisced about coming to the campus in the summer of 1968 and spending time in Quigley's. She thanked the University for the help it had provided her as first lady. And, catching the optimistic spirit of the event, she noted that, "Every time presents an opportunity to the generation that lives in it." Over the course of its generations, the University has served its students and defined its mission. It also has responded with alacrity, night and day, to the needs of its students, to the city, its federal host, and ultimately, to the nation.

As the first lady spoke to the large crowd on that pleasant spring day in the back yard that she shared with the University, one had the feeling that this was GW's time, that the promise of a college begun almost 175 years ago had been realized. And that, just over the horizon, lay the promise of an even brighter future in the generations to come.

(Above) The academic procession is a commencement tradition.

(Right) May 1993 graduates celebrating the end of their college careers and sharing high hopes for the future.

(Below) First Lady Hillary Rodham Clinton addressed graduates at the May 8, 1994, commencement. She is shown here with GW President Trachtenberg.

Presidents of the University

William Staughton 1821-1827

Stephen Chapin 1828-1841

Joel Smith Bacon 1843-1854

Joseph Getchell Binney 1855-1858

George Whitefield Samson 1859-1871

James Clarke Welling 1871-1894

Samuel Harrison Greene, *Acting* 1894-1895

Benaiah L. Whitman 1895-1900

Samuel Harrison Greene, *Acting* 1900-1902

Charles Willis Needham 1902-1910

Charles Herbert Stockton 1910-1918

William Miller Collier 1918-1921

Howard L. Hodgkins, *ad interim* 1921-1923

William Mather Lewis 1923-1927

Cloyd Heck Marvin 1927-1959

Oswald Symister Colclough, *Acting* 1959-1961

Thomas Henry Carroll 1961-1964

Oswald Symister Colclough, *Acting* 1964-1965

Lloyd Hartman Elliott 1965-1988

Stephen Joel Trachtenberg 1988-

Note: There was no president from
October 5, 1841, to October 30, 1843.

Chairmen of the Board of Trustees

Obadiah B. Brown 1821-1827

Robert B. Semple 1827-1832

Samuel Cornelius 1832-1838

James L. Edwards 1838-1867

Amos Kendall 1867-1869

William W. Corcoran 1869-1888

James Clarke Welling 1888-1894

Samuel Harrison Greene 1894-1895

Benaiah L. Whitman 1895-1900

Samuel Harrison Greene 1900-1902

Wayne MacVeagh 1902-1907

Henry Brown Floyd MacFarland 1907-1910

John Bell Larner 1910-1931

Arthur Peter, Acting 1931-1937

Robert Vedder Fleming 1937-1959

Newell Windom Ellison 1959-1965

Edward Karrick Morris 1965-1972

Charles E. Phillips 1972-1978

Glen A. Wilkinson 1978-1985

Everett H. Bellows 1985-1988

Oliver T. Carr, Jr. 1988-1995

John D. Zeglis 1995-

Note: Between 1821 and 1872, the title of the chief officer
of the Board of Trustees was President of the Board of
Trustees. The title President of the Corporation was in use
from 1872 to 1900, when the nomenclature changed to the
present Chairman of the Board of Trustees.

Photography Credits

Associated Press, 18

Adam Auel, 200

The Bettman Archive, 62-63

J.R. Black, 103

The Boston Globe, 174-175
(reprinted courtesy of *The Boston Globe*)

Peg Callihan, 179 (lower), 195

William Campbell/Time Magazine, 93

Elisabeth Casey, 199 (upper)

Cherry Tree, 27, 35 (lower), 40 (lower), 151

The Chicago Tribune, 108, 130-131 (copyright
Chicago Tribune Company. All rights reserved.
Used with permission.)

Bill Denison, 168, 193

The George Washington University Archives,
7 (lower), 8, 9, 10, 11 (upper), 12, 13, 14, 15, 16,
17, 26 (lower right), 28-29, 30 (center and lower),
31, 32, 33, 34, 35, 37, 38, 39, 40 (upper), 41, 42,
43, 46, 47, 48-49, 50, 51, 54, 55, 56, 57, 64, 65,
66, 67, 68, 71, 74, 75, 76, 77, 79, 80, 81, 82, 83,
85, 87, 88, 102 (upper), 110, 115, 116-117, 118,
121, 122-123, 124-125, 132, 134, 141, 145, 146,
147, 152, 163, 164

The George Washington University Department
of Athletics and Recreation, 52-53, 104-105, 135,
204 (upper)

The George Washington University Graduate
School of Education and Human Development,
143, 153, 154

The George Washington University Office of
University Relations, 86, 92, 111, 139, 144, 155,
157, 160

The George Washington University School of
Business and Public Management, 165, 167

Sloan Ginn, 178 (lower), 185 (lower), 187

Jon Goell, 9

Hameed Gorani, 90 (upper), 97, 112, 177

Mark Gulezian, frontispiece

Don Hamerman, 147

Nathaniel Harari, 189 (lower)

Harris & Ewing, 84

Peter A. Harris/*The Washington Times*, 142

The Hatchet, 100-101, 114, 120

David Hathcox, 19, 161, 172, 173, 181, 182, 183,
185 (upper), 186 (left), 207

John T. Hill, 61, 95, 192, 196, 198, 199 (lower), 206

Marvin Ickow, 106-107

Mitchell Layton, 202, 203, 205

Library of Congress, 7 (upper), 109 (lower)

Charles Magnus, University Collection, 22-23

Lenore Miller, 128

Lanny Nagler, 197 (right)

Bob Narod, 59 (upper), 60, 89 (lower), 91, 94, 99,
180, 189 (upper), 191, 193, 194, 197 (upper), 201

NASA, 58, 166

National Archives—Matthew Brady Collection,
20-21, 23 (upper), 26 (left)

National Portrait Gallery—Benjamin J. Falk,
89 (upper)

National Library of Science, 26 (upper right),
30 (upper)

The New York Times Company, 44-45
(reprinted by permission, copyright 1954 by
The New York Times Company)

Rick Reinhard, 96, 196 (left)

Sam Silverstein, 188

Time, Inc., 70 (© 1965 Time Inc. reprinted
by permission)

University Collection, 26 (upper right), 30 (upper),
102 (lower), 109 (upper), 126-127

The Washington Post, 72-73 (copyright 1964,
reprinted with permission), 148 (copyright 1980,
reprinted with permission)

Washingtoniana Collection, 11 (lower)

The White House, 159, 169

Amy Wilton, 136-137, 204 (lower)

Tom Wolff, 98, 150

Bibliography

French, Roderick, ed. *An Independent Institution in a Free Society: Essays in Honor of Lloyd H. Elliott, President of The George Washington University, 1965-1988*. Washington, D.C., 1988.

Hill, Peter. *The Elliott School of International Affairs: A History of International Studies at The George Washington University.*

Kayser, Elmer L. *Bricks Without Straw: The Evolution of George Washington University*. New York, 1970.

Kayser, Elmer L. *A Medical Center: The Institutional Development of Medical Education in George Washington University*. Washington, D.C., 1973.

Kayser, Elmer L. *Luther Rice, Founder of Columbian College*. Washington, D.C., 1966.

Trachtenberg, Stephen Joel. *Speaking His Mind*. Phoenix, Ariz., 1994.

The George Washington University, Office of the University Historian. *The George Washington University, 1821-1966*. Washington, D.C., 1966.

The George Washington University, Office of the University Historian. *Washington's Bequest to a National University*. Washington, D.C., 1965.

The George Washington University. *GW Magazine*. Alumni magazine that frequently covers aspects of GW's history.

The George Washington University, University Archives and Records. *Preserving GW's History*. Short bulletins dealing with various aspects of GW's history.

Index